# SPORTS COLLECTIBLES FOR FUN & PROFIT

## William C. Ketchum, Jr.

HPBooks ®

Publisher: Rick Bailey
Editorial Director: Randy Summerlin
Editor: Jacqueline Sharkey
Art Director: Don Burton
Book Manufacture: Anthony B. Narducci
Typography: Cindy Coatsworth, Michelle Carter
Consultant: Mike McDonald, The Sports Page,
              1680 N. Country Club, Tucson, AZ

Published by HPBooks, Inc.
P.O. Box 5367
Tucson, AZ 85703
602-888-2150
ISBN: 0-89586-249-2
Library of Congress
   Catalog Card Number: 85-80130
©1985 HPBooks, Inc.
Printed in U.S.A.
1st Printing

Prepared for HPBooks by Sophia Books/Layla Productions, Inc.
Publisher: Carol Paradis
Designer: Allan Mogel

The author would like to thank the following who lent assistance
and permission to make photographs for this book:

Bartholomew Fair, Ltd., New York, New York
Jay Hyams, New York, New York
Aaron Ketchum, Rye, New York
Ian Kipp, Rye, New York
Time After Time, Danbury, Connecticut
Deborah L. Weiss, New York, New York

All photographs by Calabro Studios, except for the following:
Schecter Lee—pages 10, 45, 46-47, 49, 50

# SPORTS COLLECTIBLES FOR FUN & PROFIT

## William C. Ketchum, Jr.

Getting Started . . . . . . . . . . . . . . . . . . . . . . . . . . . . . . . . . . . . . . 4
Glossary . . . . . . . . . . . . . . . . . . . . . . . . . . . . . . . . . . . . . . . . . . . . . 6
Sports Collectibles Categories . . . . . . . . . . . . . . . . . . . . . . . . . 10
   Baseball Collectibles . . . . . . . . . . . . . . . . . . . . . . . . . . . . . . . . 11
   Football Collectibles . . . . . . . . . . . . . . . . . . . . . . . . . . . . . . . . 17
   Basketball Collectibles . . . . . . . . . . . . . . . . . . . . . . . . . . . . . . 22
   Ice-Hockey Collectibles . . . . . . . . . . . . . . . . . . . . . . . . . . . . . 24
   Golf Collectibles . . . . . . . . . . . . . . . . . . . . . . . . . . . . . . . . . . . 25
   Tennis Collectibles . . . . . . . . . . . . . . . . . . . . . . . . . . . . . . . . . 28
   Fishing Collectibles . . . . . . . . . . . . . . . . . . . . . . . . . . . . . . . . 32
   Hunting Collectibles . . . . . . . . . . . . . . . . . . . . . . . . . . . . . . . . 37
   Duck and Shore-Bird Decoys . . . . . . . . . . . . . . . . . . . . . . . . 44
   Fish Decoys, Jigs and Spears . . . . . . . . . . . . . . . . . . . . . . . . 49
   Bicycling, Ice-Skating, Roller-
      Skating and Skiing Collectibles . . . . . . . . . . . . . . . . . . . . 51
   Other Sports Collectibles . . . . . . . . . . . . . . . . . . . . . . . . . . . 55
Building a Collection . . . . . . . . . . . . . . . . . . . . . . . . . . . . . . . . . 60
Price Guide . . . . . . . . . . . . . . . . . . . . . . . . . . . . . . . . . . . . . . . . . 74
Bibliography . . . . . . . . . . . . . . . . . . . . . . . . . . . . . . . . . . . . . . . . 94
Index . . . . . . . . . . . . . . . . . . . . . . . . . . . . . . . . . . . . . . . . . . . . . . . 95

# Getting Started

Americans love sports, and collecting sports memorabilia is one of this country's fastest-growing hobbies. Each sport has its enthusiasts and collectibles. Football fans collect player cards; fishing enthusiasts buy rods and reels; golfers look for old clubs; and tennis players are interested in antique rackets. You can find numerous collectibles for any sport.

## WONDERFUL BARGAINS

Sports collectibles are popular for many reasons. One is that so many types of mementos are available. Because these mementos have changed over the years, you can assemble an extensive collection for any sport.

Most sports memorabilia are also inexpensive. Even though you can pay $15,000 or more for a special duck decoy or a rare Kentucky rifle, thousands of fascinating items cost less than $1 each.

This book shows you how to evaluate sports memorabilia. As with all collectibles, price is important. How much should you pay for a ticket to the 1926 World Series? How much should you pay for a horseshoe once worn by the famous racehorse Whirlaway? The price guide in this book provides information for determining the value of all types of collectibles, from 50-cent baseball cards to yachting trophies.

## A SECTION FOR EVERY SPORT

Each of the following sections covers one or more fields of sports memorabilia. The introduction to each section gives you important facts about the sport and its collectibles.

Each field includes both common, inexpensive items and rare, costly ones. This book provides information about both types. Even if you don't plan to collect expensive items, you should learn about them. You may be lucky and find a duck decoy by a master carver such as Lemuel Ward. Or you may find a rare Currier & Ives print of the legendary trotter Hambletonian. This book will enable you to recognize such rarities and to evaluate their worth.

## JOYS OF COLLECTING

Collecting is a social activity. Because you will probably want to meet other enthusiasts, this book provides information about collectors' organizations. It also discusses antique shows, auctions and shops. They offer you opportunities to meet people who share your interests. As your collection grows, so will your circle of friends.

Caring for a collection requires skill and patience. New acquisitions have to be cleaned. Some must be repaired. All should be catalogued and insured. Photographing your collection is also a good idea. This book discusses these matters in a simple, practical way.

Collecting is more fun when it is shared. Many collectors are eager to show their acquisitions to family, friends and other collectors. However, they don't know safe, attractive ways to display their pieces. This book discusses proper display and storage techniques. It also discusses ways to prevent theft and damage.

This book includes all the information you need to become a sports memorabilia collector. As you become more involved, you may wish to learn more about a specific field. The bibliography in this book can help you decide what to read next.

A book should make your search for collectibles more fun and rewarding. It should also help you save money. The more time you invest learning about your chosen area, the less money you will spend. The wiser you become, the more chance you will have of finding a rare, valuable piece. This is every collector's dream—and yours may come true!

The term *sports collectibles* covers various types of
memorabilia.

# Glossary

**America's Cup**—Trophy awarded to winner of race between American yacht and that of a foreign nation. The America's Cup was won by a foreign competitor for the first time in 1983.

**Appraisal**—Estimate of the value of a collectible.

**Arkansas toothpick**—See *Bowie knife.*

**Awards**—See *Trophies.*

**Bag**—A day's catch of fish or game.

**Batteries**—Wood rafts that commercial hunters mounted cast-iron decoys on.

**Battery decoys**—Cast-iron decoys used in commercial hunting. The practice was outlawed in 1918. These decoys could not float, so hunters mounted them on wood rafts called *batteries.*

**Beaters**—People who walk ahead of hunters and stir up game.

**Bird**—See *shuttlecock.*

**Bobbers**—Devices used to float fishing bait in the water.

**Bolts**—Short arrows fired from a crossbow.

**Bone crusher**—High-wheeled 19th-century bicycle with solid rubber tires and no springs.

**Bore**—Inside diameter of a firearm.

**Bowie knife**—An 18-inch knife used to skin and cut up dead game. This knife was also used for protection, and to kill buffalo from horseback. Also called an *Arkansas toothpick.*

**Brassies**—Early golf clubs known today as *No. 2 woods.*

**Breech-loading**—Guns that are loaded behind the barrel.

**Brick**—A group of collectors' cards sold as a unit.

**Buffalo guns**—Rifles used by buffalo hunters.

**Bull's-eye**—The circular central mark on archery or rifle targets.

**Cane**—Asian bamboo used in 19th-century fly rods.

**Capote**—Heavy cape used by a matador in the first stages of a bullfight.

**Cartridge**—Ammunition consisting of a bullet, powder and primer, all enclosed in a metal case. Cartridges are used in rifles and handguns.

**Casting lure**—Bait that pulls the fishing line from the reel when the line is cast. These lures are heavier and larger than spinning lures.

**Casting reel**—Fishing line is wound around the spool of this reel. When the line is cast, the weight of the lure pulls the line, forcing the spool to revolve. This type of reel is also called a *Kentucky reel.*

**Casting rod**—Short rod used in bait casting. The line is propelled by the weight of the lure.

**Closed-face reels**—Fly reels with solid sides. Some fly reels have perforated sides, which reduce the weight of the reel and provide ventilation to dry the line.

**Composition**—A material made of paper, wood pulp and glue. It is used in factory-made decoys.

**Confidence decoy**—Wood or wood-and-cork replica of a swan or gull. These waterfowl cannot be hunted. The idea is that when ducks see the replica floating on the water, they think it is safe to land.

**Creel**—Wood, wicker, bamboo or cloth bag with shoulder strap. Fishermen carry their catches in creels.

**Crossbow**—Bow set on a stock that fires short arrows called *bolts.* Some crossbows are cocked with a crank.

**Cue**—Tapered, leather-tipped stick used to strike billiards balls.

**Drivers**—Early golf clubs known today as *No. 1 woods.*

**Duck decoy**—A wood or wood-and-cork replica designed to attract waterfowl within range of a hunter's

The technical term for items such as these bullfighting posters, programs and tickets is *ephemera.*

weapon. Unlike shore-bird decoys, duck decoys float.

**Duck stamps**—Federal and state licensing stamps issued to hunters for a fee.

**Ebonized**—Wood or metal that has been painted or enameled black to resemble ebony wood.

**Epee**—A thin-pointed dueling sword without a cutting edge. It resembles a foil, but is heavier and more rigid.

**Ephemera**—Collectible paper goods, including periodicals, ticket stubs and posters.

**Error card**—Collector card with a printing mistake, such as a misspelled word or an incorrect color.

**Facsimile signatures**—Copies of players' signatures that manufacturers stamp on sports equipment. Such signatures do not add to the value of an item, as a genuine autograph does.

**Fair**—Collectors' term for an item showing substantial damage or wear, including loss of minor parts.

**Fanzine**—Periodical devoted to the special interests of one group of fans.

**Fine**—Collectors' term for an undamaged item showing slight signs of wear.

**Flies**—Bits of feather, floss and tinsel used to attract fish. Flies are made to resemble bugs and minnows.

**Flintlock**—Early gunlock in which a flint in the hammer struck a metal plate, producing a spark that ignited the powder.

**Floating decoy**—Flat-bottomed decoy used on water. It is anchored by a line connected to a weight.

**Fly rod**—Long, slim rod of wood, metal or graphite used for casting trout and salmon flies.

**Foil**—A long, thin dueling sword with a button on the point to prevent injury.

**Fly reel**—A reel used to store the fly line.

**Game**—Wild birds, fish or animals hunted for sport or for use as food. The taking of game is usually regulated by state or federal laws.

**Gauge**—Measurement of the inside diameter, or *bore,* of a shotgun. Most shotguns range in gauge from 12 to 20.

**Giveaways**—Novelty items (such as pins or cards) inserted in packages of cigarettes, gum, ice cream or other products to increase sales. Many are collectible.

**Good**—Collectors' term for an item showing wear and age but no serious damage.

**Go-withs**—Items that accompany a piece of sports equipment. Tennis-racket presses and covers are go-withs.

**Green's-level gauges**—Devices that measure the slope of a golf green.

**Gunning equipment**—Variety of items used by hunters. Includes such things as powder horns, hunting knives and cleaning tools.

**Hallmark**—Manufacturer's mark on a gold, silver or pewter piece.

**Handguns**—Guns with barrels less than 8 inches long.

**High-ticket item**—A high-priced memento.

**How-to book**—Book that explains how to play a sport.

**Ivory**—Hard, white, bony substance from whale, elephant or walrus.

**Jigs**—Lead or copper objects used to catch fish. Some are shaped like fish; others are triangular or rectangular. They usually have one or more hooks attached to one end.

**Kentucky reel**—Early form of free-spool casting reel made in the Lexington, Kentucky area.

**Kentucky rifles**—Long-barreled rifles made between 1750 and 1850. They were usually beautifully decorated and very accurate. Most Kentucky rifles were made in Pennsylvania.

**La fiesta brava**—Spanish term for *bullfight.*

**Leg**—The stick that holds a shore-bird decoy upright in sand or mud.

**Long guns**—Guns with barrels more than 8 inches long. These guns, which include rifles and shotguns, are used for hunting.

This bicycle, called a *bone crusher,* is rare and expensive.

**Lures**—Wood, metal or plastic bait used in fishing. Lures are made to resemble fish, frogs or other small creatures.

**Man traps**—Devices used by European landowners in the 18th and 19th centuries to protect their estates from poachers. These devices could cause serious injury.

**Matchlock**—Early gunlock in which the powder charge was ignited by a slow-burning wick or cord.

**Medals**—Small, flat metal awards given for outstanding performances in such sports as track. Medals often have an attached silk ribbon.

**Mint**—Collectors' term for an undamaged item showing no visible signs of wear.

**Muleta**—A small cloth cape used by a matador during the last stages of a bullfight.

**Multiplying reel**—A type of casting reel. When a fisherman turns the handle once, the spool turns two, three or four times. Multiplying reels draw in the line faster than other types.

**Muzzle-loading**—Guns that are loaded through the muzzle.

**Nine pins**—A form of bowling popular in New York City in the 17th century.

**Ordinary**—19th-century bicycle with a very large front wheel and a small rear wheel.

**Peeps**—Another term for shore birds such as sandpipers and curlews.

**Pennant**—Triangular cloth flag bearing the name of football, basketball, baseball or hockey team.

**Penny farthing**—English name for bicycle known in this country as the *ordinary.*

**Percussion cap**—Small paper or metal container that held a charge and exploded when struck.

**Plains rifles**—Short-barreled rifles that could be easily handled on horseback.

**Plinkers**—Early, octagonal-barrel .22-caliber guns used for small game and target shooting.

**Plugs**—Type of bait first made in the mid-19th century. Early plugs were fish-shaped and were made of carved, painted wood. They had metal fins, propellers and devices to make them sink or wobble. Later plugs have plastic bodies.

**Poaching**—To hunt or catch fish or game illegally. Poaching usually involves trespassing.

**Pocket cap**—Metal base at the end of the handle of a fishing rod.

**Poona**—East Indian game from which badminton was derived in the 19th century.

**Poor**—Collectors' term for a badly damaged item. Substantial parts of the item may be missing.

**Powder horn**—Hollow cow horn plugged at each end with a piece of wood. It was used to carry black powder for guns in the days before cartridges.

**Provenance**—The history of an object.

**Punch board**—A gambling device. Some featured pictures of baseball players.

**Racing silks**—Caps and blouses worn by jockeys or sulky drivers.

**Rack**—A pair of antlers.

**Racquets**—Forerunner of squash and tennis.

**Rapier**—A light, sharp-pointed dueling sword used only for thrusting.

**Reel**—Circular frame, usually made of metal, set on the handle of a fishing rod. Fishermen use the reel to store line and to let the line in or out.

**Riding crop**—Wood or leather whip with a looped lash and a short stock. Riders use a crop to encourage a horse to go faster.

**Rifling**—Cutting spiral grooves on the inside of a gun's barrel to make the bullet spin when fired. The spinning gives the bullet greater accuracy and distance.

**Roller polo**—Early ice-hockeylike game played on roller skates.

**Run**—Group of consecutively numbered collectors' cards or publications.

**Saber**—A dueling sword used with a slashing as well as a thrusting movement. In fencing, competitors can score points by touching opponents with the edge or the point of the saber.

**Shore-bird decoy**—Wood or wood-and-cork replica of one of the long-legged birds that live along saltwater beaches. Unlike duck decoys, shore-bird decoys do not float. They are fitted with a long stick, or *leg*, which is stuck in sand or mud. This type of decoy is also called a *stickup decoy*.

**Shot shell**—Shotgun ammunition usually enclosed in a paper or plastic skin.

**Shuttlecock**—Object that players hit with a racket in badminton. Also called a *bird*. Early examples had real feathers and cork-and-rubber bases.

**Silhouette decoy**—A decoy made from a flat board and painted on both sides. Hunters mount two or three silhouettes on a platform to keep the decoys upright in the water. Examples used for dry-land shooting are mounted on sticks.

**Single-action reel**—This reel is usually used with a fly rod. When a fisherman turns the handle, the spool revolves once. These reels are designed primarily to hold fishing line.

**Spinner**—Type of metal bait first made in the mid-19th century. A spinner consists of propeller-shaped bits of metal mounted on a shaft. It spins as it is pulled through the water.

**Spinning lures**—Bait that pulls the fishing line from the reel when the line is cast. These lures are smaller and lighter than casting lures.

**Spinning reel**—A reel whose spool does not revolve when the fishing line is cast.

**Spinning rod**—Fairly long metal or graphite rod used with a spinning reel to cast extra-light lures.

**Spoon**—Type of metal bait first made in the mid-19th century. A spoon is egg-shaped and wobbles as it is pulled through the water.

**Spoons**—Early golf clubs known today as *No. 3 woods*.

**Sporting artist**—Artist who specializes in paintings, photographs or sculptures related to sports.

**Sporting firearms**—Guns designed for hunting.

**Stickup decoy**—See *shore-bird decoy*.

**Stirrups**—Circular rings with flat bottoms hung by a strap from a saddle. Riders place their feet in stirrups when mounting or riding.

**Stymie marker**—A device golfers use to indicate the position of the ball when the ball must be picked up.

**Suit of lights**—Matador's costume. Called *traje de luces* in Spanish.

**Sulky**—Horse-drawn carriage used in pacing and trotting races.

**Swap fests**—Events at collectors' conventions during which enthusiasts buy, sell and exchange mementos.

**Tack**—Equipment used in horseback riding. Includes saddles and bridles.

**Tackle**—Equipment used by fishermen. Includes storage boxes, nets, creels and lure cases.

**Team sports**—Sports participated in by groups rather than individuals. For example, baseball is a team sport.

**The courting game**—Another term for croquet.

**Tip up**—Signaling device used by ice fishermen. This Y-shaped wood device has a spring-loaded cotton flag. The fisherman puts the device on the edge of a hole in the ice, then runs a line through it. When a fish takes the bait and runs, it triggers the spring and the flag pops up.

**Traje de luces**—See *suit of lights*.

**Trophies**—Awards, usually shaped like a cup, given for outstanding performances. The term also refers to preserved and mounted animal horns or body parts.

**Velocipede**—Early 19th-century bicycle. The word is Latin for *speedy foot*.

**Wheel lock**—Early gunlock in which a rough wheel was spun on a flint to throw sparks that set off the charge.

**Wheel skating**—Early name for roller skating.

**Wheelmen**—Members of 19th-century bicycling clubs.

**Working decoy**—A decoy designed for hunters rather than collectors.

Fishing reels.

# Sports Collectibles Categories

Americans participate in and follow many sports. Our passion for sports is matched by our passion for collecting sports memorabilia. As you read this book, you will see that most sports have collectibles associated with them. There is something for everyone.

## CATEGORIES OF COLLECTING

This book divides sports memorabilia into categories. These categories have been established by collectors. Most categories are based on specific sports. You will find chapters on baseball memorabilia, football memorabilia and hunting memorabilia.

Sports memorabilia can also be categorized by the material from which the items are made. For example, some enthusiasts buy only paper collectibles.

Some items are classified by their original function. Some people collect only duck decoys.

Some categories overlap. Collectors' cards are available for several sports. Most card collectors acquire cardboard portraits of major-league baseball, football, basketball and hockey players. Such cards are usually sold with chewing gum. In the past, they were sold with tobacco and other items. Thousands of these cards are available. You can buy cards showing players of one sport, such as baseball, or you can buy cards showing players of different sports.

Some sports have only a few types of collectibles. Others have many. For example, duck hunting offers fewer possibilities than other sports. Enthusiasts can collect shotguns, game bags or the stamps required on bird-hunting permits. They can also buy carved wood replicas of ducks, geese, swans and other birds.

Horseracing has extensive memorabilia. Collectors can buy racing saddles and other riding equipment. They can also buy paper memorabilia such as racing programs, betting stubs, admission tickets and newspaper articles about famous racehorses.

These finely carved shore-bird decoys were made between 1915 and 1918. At left and right are representations of the ruddy turnstone, $250 to $750 each. In the center is a greater yellowlegs, by the well-known carver A. Elmer Crowell. It is worth $1,700 to $3,200.

The categories in this book are based on popular taste. Use them as guidelines. Collect what you like. If you are interested in several fields, collect items from each. The best collection is one that is personally rewarding.

## AMERICAN-MADE OR FOREIGN-MADE COLLECTIBLES

Many categories in this book include foreign-made items. Some are very interesting and make your collection more valuable. Hunting, fishing and horseracing have numerous foreign-made items. Remember that you do not need to follow any rules except those that you create for yourself. Some categories, such as bullfighting, are composed almost entirely of foreign-made items.

# BASEBALL COLLECTIBLES

Among the most popular sports memorabilia are items associated with baseball, America's national pastime. Baseball reportedly was created by Abner Doubleday in Cooperstown, New York, in 1839. The first rule book was printed in 1858. The sport was popular with Union soldiers during the Civil War.

If you want a category with many possibilities, baseball will interest you. Because the sport has existed nearly 150 years, many collectibles are available. These items range from equipment to paper collectibles. An estimated 1 billion baseball cards have been issued. Thousands of programs and admission tickets have been printed. Most baseball collectibles were made in the 20th century, but you can also find many 19th-century items.

Baseball offers so many types of memorabilia that you will probably want to concentrate on one category. You might collect equipment; books and periodicals; *ephemera* or paper items; or cards and souvenirs.

## BASEBALL EQUIPMENT

Baseball equipment includes wood bats, horsehide- or cowhide-covered balls, bases, padded gloves and protective gear for catchers. The design of each item has changed continually, so you can buy many different styles.

Some collectors acquire only baseball bats. Others specialize in balls, gloves, or catchers' masks and pads. Some collect shoes or uniforms. Others collect the lockers in which players stored all this gear!

Some enthusiasts collect every bat or glove; others acquire the products of one manufacturer. Well-known manufacturers include H. J. Wilson Co., Baton Rouge, Louisiana; Rawlings Sporting Goods Co., St. Louis; Spalding, Chicopee, Massachusetts; and Hillerich & Bradsby, maker of the famous Louisville Slugger bats. Since the 1950s, a great deal of baseball equipment has been made in foreign countries, especially Taiwan and Japan. However, most collectors focus on earlier, American-made products.

The most eagerly sought pieces are those that were worn or used by major-league players. A piece of gear owned by a star such as Ty Cobb costs hundreds or thousands of dollars. Such items are rare.

Collectors also prize autographed equipment.

Miniature plastic batting helmets are a popular collectible. The large examples were ice-cream containers and sell for $2 to $3. The small ones were sold in vending machines and now cost 50 cents to 75 cents. Buy these items now. Their value will increase.

Baseball team pennants are interesting and inexpensive. Examples made between 1930 and 1980 cost $3 to $20 each. Look for pennants from teams that no longer exist, such as the Brooklyn Dodgers and the Philadelphia Athletics.

Don't be fooled by *facsimile signatures.* As early as 1912, Spalding was selling baseball bats with stamped copies of stars' signatures. Today, many bats and gloves have signatures of famous players. Genuine autographs are rarer and more valuable.

## BASEBALL BOOKS AND PERIODICALS

Hundreds of books have been written about baseball. The earliest appeared in 1866, just one year after the Civil War ended. However, the first biography of a baseball player did not appear until 1900.

Today, books about the lives and exploits of famous players are very popular with collectors. You'll find numerous books about such stars as Willie Mays, Babe Ruth and Lou Gehrig. Most baseball books were written after 1940. Books written in the 19th century are hard to find.

Magazines that published baseball stories and statistics are readily available. The earliest, *Sporting News,* was founded in 1886 and is still in business. Other popular periodicals are *Baseball Magazine,* founded in 1908 and discontinued in 1953, and *Baseball Digest.*

Some issues of these periodicals are rarer and more expensive than others. Remember that a *run* is much more valuable than an equal number of miscellaneous issues. A *run* is a group of consecutive issues of a magazine. Some collectors spend hundreds of dollars and years of effort trying to fill a long run.

The annual guides that provided information on professional players and teams are also collectible. Look for the *Beadle Baseball Guide,* founded in 1860 and discontinued in 1930. *Baseball Yearbook,* the *Little Red Book of Baseball,* the *Baseball Blue Book, Who's Who in Baseball* and the *World Series Record Book* are also well-known.

## BASEBALL EPHEMERA

If you are a baseball fan, you may have some baseball ephemera. *Ephemera* are the paper goods related to a sport. These include tickets and programs.

Many enthusiasts collect tickets or ticket stubs relating to one team or event. Tickets to the World Series or the All-Star Game are very popular. Programs sold or given away at games are also collectible. Ticket stubs or programs for games in which something important happened are especially valuable. Such events include Roger Maris' 61st home run and Ted Williams' retirement. Team yearbooks and posters are also popular with some collectors.

## BASEBALL CARDS

Baseball cards are the most popular sports memorabilia. Three factors have contributed to their success.

Not all baseball cards were issued by chewing-gum manufacturers. These examples were given away with breakfast foods. Such items are not as popular as chewing-gum cards and are harder to find. These date from 1976 to 1983 and are worth 10 cents to 25 cents each.

First, the cards are plentiful.

Second, they are issued in sets. This increases their appeal because collectors like to assemble groups of items.

Third, most cards are inexpensive. A few cards are very costly. A Honus Wagner card from about 1910 is worth $10,000. However, thousands of cards made between 1960 and 1980 cost 50 cents apiece or less.

Many fans are familiar with the cards that came with bubble gum. The standard package contained from 2 to 15 cards and a piece of gum.

However, the first baseball cards did not come with bubble gum. Some were sold with tobacco and cigarettes. Others came with the hot dogs and ice cream sold at ballparks. Even the bakeries that prepared the hot-dog rolls had their own cards. These cards were *giveaways*. They were tucked into packages of cigarettes or chewing tobacco or under the lid of a cup of ice cream.

**Goodwin & Co—**The first baseball cards appeared during the mid-1880s. The first manufacturer is believed to have been Goodwin & Co. of New York City, which made more than 2,000 cards. Other major manufacturers included the Gold Coin Chewing Tobacco Co.

**Goudey Gum Co.—**Tobacco companies led the field until the 1920s. Then candy manufacturers took the lead. In 1933, the Goudey Gum Co. of Boston produced the first bubble-gum baseball card. Goudey produced cards until 1941.

Among the novelties of the card field are these 3-D Super Star cards, made between 1969 and 1974. They appear three-dimensional when properly viewed and have facsimile signatures. These unusual collectibles cost 75 cents to $1 each.

This baseball bears facsimile signatures of the 1981 New York Yankees baseball team. Although produced in substantial quantity, such collectibles will increase in value. This example is worth $20 to $25.

These Topps cards represent the many different categories of baseball cards. Some collectors concentrate on one type, such as rookie cards.

**Bowman Co.** — This firm, located in Philadelphia, began issuing cards in 1948. Before it was bought out by the Topps Chewing Gum Co. of Brooklyn, New York, in 1955, Bowman manufactured thousands of cards.

**Topps Chewing Gum Co.** — The greatest card producer is Topps. Since entering the field with two limited sets in 1951, the company has distributed an estimated 300 million baseball cards! Most are readily available and inexpensive. However, some cards are rare and valuable. One 1952 card of the illustrious Mickey Mantle is especially prized by collectors.

Other well-known manufacturers of bubble-gum cards are Fleer Corp. of Philadelphia and The Donruss Co. of Memphis, Tenn. All produced standard cards, which include a picture of a player and important information about him.

Modern manufacturers, driven by competition and the desire to increase production, have created variations. Hundreds of new types of baseball cards appear on the market each year. Team cards are now issued. One such card has a picture of the entire 1973 Chicago Cubs roster. There are cards for Hall of Fame and All-Star team members. There is also a group called *stars*. These cards feature players who hit the most home runs, stole the most bases or set some other record.

What should you collect? Look for *error cards*. These cards have misprints, misspellings or other mistakes. They are expensive.

Cards featuring leading players are always in demand. However, thousands of these cards are produced each year. Only older, rarer cards bring high prices. A Hank Aaron card issued after he was an established star is very inexpensive. A card featuring Aaron in his rookie year is more costly.

Most collectors of post-World War II cards collect by team or league. You can also collect only All-Star cards or cards from teams in the World Series. You have many options, and they are all fun.

### BASEBALL SOUVENIRS

Even before 1900, professional teams realized they could supplement their profits by selling souvenirs to fans. Today, these mementos represent an exciting field for collectors.

Some early pieces are rare, costly and exotic. Such pieces include a folding fan embellished with pictures of the 1907 Pittsburgh Pirates team, and a Babe Ruth "Sultan of Swat" pocket watch.

Less-expensive items are available. Teams have put their names and symbols on numerous objects, all of which are collectible. These include calendars, banks, pens, pencils and clocks shaped like baseballs. Sun visors, T-shirts, paperweights, beer glasses, letter openers, cigarette lighters, dolls and key chains are available. Teams also sell caps, wastepaper baskets and rings.

Other unusual collectibles include porcelain or metal statuettes, and silver or pewter season passes. In 1908, one company produced a series of postcards featuring members of the Detroit Tigers and Cleveland Indians. In 1934 and 1935, the Diamond Match Co. of Springfield, Massachusetts, offered book matches with covers displaying portraits of contemporary stars. Some *punch boards,* or gambling devices, featured pictures of players.

Some items are costly. World Series rings, which are awarded only to participants, rarely come on the market. They are very expensive. This is understandable. Such rings are treasured by their owners.

Some souvenirs come in such variety that they can be collected as a special category. Pins and coin disks are two examples.

Metal pins appeared before 1900. They were giveaways. The pins were inserted in packs of cigarettes, gum, potato chips and cigars. Cereal and bread manufacturers also offered these premiums.

Coin disks are usually made of plastic or an inexpensive metal. They feature the portraits of well-known players.

### COLLECTING BASEBALL MEMORABILIA

Your opportunities to obtain baseball memorabilia will depend on the category you select. Baseball cards are by far the easiest memorabilia to locate. You can find them in many different places. New series are produced each year. They can be purchased with packages of chewing gum at newsstands, variety stores and supermarkets.

Other sources for baseball cards include other collectors. Get to know them and swap cards. Attend collectors' conventions, where *swap fests* are held.

You can also buy from dealers. Specialists in this field stock thousands of cards. Unless you are seeking rare examples, you can find most cards at local outlets.

Periodicals, baseball equipment and souvenirs are more elusive. Few dealers stock baseball equipment. The best way to find such items is to advertise. Old baseball gloves, bats and bases sometimes show up at flea markets, yard sales and secondhand stores.

The best sources for periodicals are secondhand book or magazine dealers. Such dealers stock back issues of all types of periodicals.

Ephemera is more difficult to locate. Some ticket stubs and programs are carried by dealers of sports memorabilia or baseball cards. Stubs and programs are also available from general ephemera dealers. These dealers stock items such as yearbooks, trading cards, advertising posters and sheet music.

# FOOTBALL COLLECTIBLES

The first college football game was played in New Brunswick, New Jersey, in 1869. However, professional teams were not organized until the 20th century. As a result, both college and professional memorabilia are popular. This is not the case with other sports. For example, only professional baseball and hockey teams' memorabilia are collectible.

Football memorabilia are similar to baseball mementos. However, the quantities and types of football memorabilia are more limited. Equipment is the one exception.

In addition, football items are less expensive than baseball mementos. Although football is the No. 1 television sports attraction, most sports-memorabilia enthusiasts prefer baseball. Therefore, prices for baseball items are higher. Collectors' cards are a good example. A rare baseball card may cost $10,000, but the rarest football card costs a few hundred dollars.

The basic collecting categories are equipment, books and periodicals, ephemera, cards and souvenirs.

## FOOTBALL EQUIPMENT

Some enthusiasts seek every item related to football. They buy uniforms, shoes, pennants and Super Bowl ticket stubs. However, most collectors buy footballs and helmets.

Footballs are often autographed, either by an individual or by a team. Make sure you are buying genuine signatures and not facsimiles. For decades, facsimile signatures have been applied to footballs. Such signatures are designed to make youngsters believe that the ball will enable them to pass like Joe Theismann or run like Tony Dorsett.

Helmets are sometimes autographed, especially by defensive players. Early helmets were small, lightly padded and made of leather. Later examples are larger, have complex face guards and are made of plastic.

Jerseys worn by important collegiate or professional players are collectible.

As with baseball, the major equipment manufacturers include Wilson, Spalding and Rawlings. The age of an item has less effect on value than its history. A 19th-century helmet of unknown origin is not nearly as valuable as a more recent one worn by Jim Brown.

## FOOTBALL BOOKS AND PERIODICALS

Many football books are available. Most were printed after 1940 and sell for less than $40. Even a classic such as Walter Camp's *American Football,* published in 1891, costs less than $175.

Several periodicals are available. These include guides, such as *Spalding's Football Guide,* published from 1885 to 1937, and the *National Collegiate Athletic Association Official Football Guide.* Annual publications such as the *True Football Yearbook* and the *Illustrated Football Annual,* issued from 1930 to 1943, are collectible.

You can also buy media guides issued by profes-

This Coca-Cola bottle is an unusual collectible made for Super Bowl XVIII. Both sides are shown. Although it was made in 1984, this collectible is already worth $5 to $10.

sional football teams. Super Bowl guides are the most valuable.

## FOOTBALL EPHEMERA

Football ephemera includes ticket stubs, programs and posters. More collegiate than professional examples are available. The most popular collectors' items are those produced for the Super Bowl.

Most collectors buy pieces pertaining to a specific team or conference. Many enthusiasts also concentrate on specific years. For example, they collect ephemera associated with the Big 10 conference during the 1950s. This enables an enthusiast to assemble a more complete collection. Such collections are more valuable than individual items in similar condition.

## FOOTBALL CARDS

Football runs a poor second to baseball in regard to collectors' cards. The first baseball cards were made before 1900. It was not until 1933 that the first football cards appeared. And these early examples were only part of a general athletic series called *Sports Kings,* produced by the Goudey Gum Co.

**National Chicle Co.**—The National Chicle Co. issued the first complete football set in 1935. It was 13 years before another firm, Bowman, entered the field.

**Bowman Co.**—This firm originally manufactured baseball cards. After it began issuing football cards, other companies entered the field. Today, thousands of cards are available.

**Topps Chewing Gum Co.**—The most important manufacturer in this field, as in baseball, is the Topps Chewing Gum Co. Topps began with cards featuring collegiate players in 1950. The company began featuring professional players after buying out Bowman in 1955. Its annual set now exceeds 500 cards.

Other important manufacturers include Fleer, which documented the American Football League from 1960 to 1963. Since 1968, The O PEE CHEE Co. has offered cards showing Canadian Football League players. The cards' text is in French and English.

Collectors can buy fewer types of football cards than baseball cards. Most football examples show one player and provide his statistics. Team cards are also available. The most valuable cards are those showing Super Bowl and Hall of Fame players and superstars during their rookie year.

Many types of football collectibles are available. Examples shown here include a football autographed by the great running back Gale Sayers, $100 to $125; the 1931 Huddle football game, $35 to $45; a set of 1981 collectors' cards featuring the Dallas Cowboys cheerleaders, $1 to $2 each.

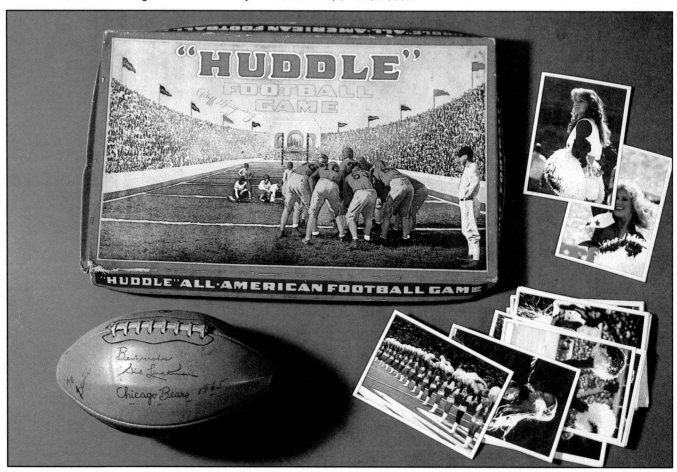

T-shirts and other clothing and equipment associated with professional football teams are collectible. These T-shirts feature the Baltimore (now Indianapolis) Colts; the New York Giants; and the company filming National Football League games. These mementos cost $15 to $40 each.

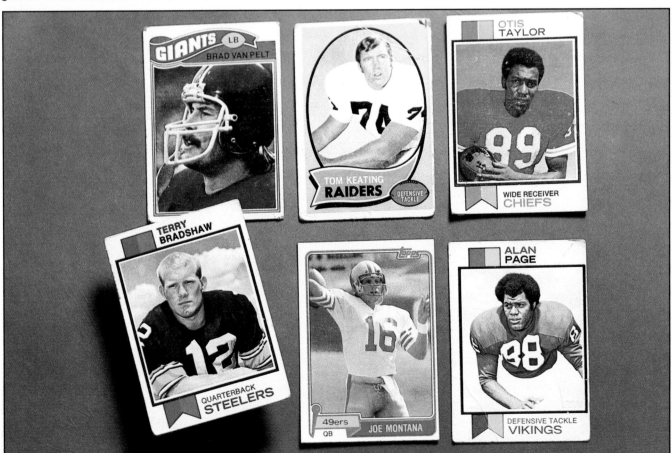

Football cards issued by the Topps Chewing Gum Co., Brooklyn, New York, are inexpensive and easy to find. These examples date from 1969 to 1980 and cost 25 cents to 75 cents each.

These leather bookmarks, made between 1920 and 1930, are hard to find. They are worth $1 to $4 each.

## FOOTBALL SOUVENIRS

The most popular collegiate football souvenir from the period before World War II is the pennant. Every school had one, and dormitory rooms were festooned with pennants of conference rivals.

However, most collectors concentrate on souvenirs associated with professional teams. These include hats, caps (once popular with collegiate teams) and T-shirts.

Press kits issued to media representatives are also popular, but are harder to find. Such kits include pens, pencils, paperweights, notebooks and tote bags. All are marked with team or league symbols. Similar items are sold to the public.

Other popular souvenirs include press pins, ashtrays, cigarette lighters, glasses and miniature helmets.

Some helmets are sold with ice cream. Others are available from vending machines.

Players' shoulder patches are also collectible. Patches worn by Super Bowl players are the most valuable.

## COLLECTING FOOTBALL MEMORABILIA

Many dealers selling baseball memorabilia also sell football mementos. Collectors' conventions usually have both football and baseball cards.

Many football cards are not as old or rare as baseball cards. Football cards were first made during the 1930s, and 90% were issued after 1950. It is possible, although difficult, to assemble a complete collection of football cards. Collectors attempting this usually contact specialized dealers, who watch for needed items.

General memorabilia dealers also stock football mementos. Dealers handling items made between 1940 and 1960 are usually very helpful.

Items connected with the Super Bowl have the greatest collector appeal.

The field of football memorabilia is less competitive than that of baseball memorabilia. As a result, collectors with limited funds have greater opportunities.

---

### BUYING AND SELLING FOOTBALL COLLECTIBLES

- Early college football equipment, such as helmets, pads and cleats, can be a good investment. You can learn about such equipment by reading books on football history and studying the pictures. Because few collectors are interested in these items, prices are low.
- High school or college gyms and locker rooms are good places to look for football memorabilia. Equipment made before 1950 was often stored when it became obsolete. You won't find this type of gear at yard sales. It wasn't until after World War II that people could afford to buy their children protective equipment.
- College and professional football pennants are interesting collectibles. Remember that most are wool. Store them with mothballs.

---

Super Bowl jewelry available to collectors includes this gold-filled Super Bowl XII necklace, $70 to $95; a silver-plated Super Bowl XVIII pin, $25 to $30; an NBC Sports pin for Super Bowl XVII, $35 to $45; and a stickpin crowned with the Super Bowl trophy, $40 to $55.

# BASKETBALL COLLECTIBLES

Basketball is one of America's favorite spectator sports. Its popularity is exceeded only by that of baseball and football.

Basketball did not develop from other activities, as most sports did. The game was invented in 1891 by a Springfield, Massachusetts, YMCA teacher named James Naismith. He wanted a game his students could play indoors during bad weather. The equipment for his new sport included peach baskets attached to the gymnasium walls.

Basketball has come a long way since then. Today, millions of fans thrill to the lightning pace of the modern game. And where there are fans, there are collectors.

Some enthusiasts are interested in mementos of college basketball. Items related to the National Collegiate Athletic Association and National Invitational Tournament championships are especially popular.

However, most collectors seek objects associated with the professional leagues.

Major collecting categories include equipment, ephemera and cards.

## BASKETBALL EQUIPMENT

Basketballs are the most popular collectibles. Examples made before 1910 and those with autographs of well-known players are especially valuable. Any uniform associated with the National Basketball Association (NBA) has some value. Uniforms are also collectible. A uniform worn by Jerry West or Bill Bradley is worth hundreds of dollars. Shoes and warm-up jackets are also collectible.

## BASKETBALL EPHEMERA

Basketball ephemera includes programs, ticket stubs and posters. The most valuable items are those printed for the NBA playoffs and championship. Press guides for NBA teams, which have been published since the 1960s, interest many collectors.

Enthusiasts also buy items related to the former American Basketball Association (ABA). However, such items are worth less than those associated with the NBA. Paper goods featuring ABA players who became NBA stars are especially valuable. One such player is Julius Erving, known as "Dr. J."

## BASKETBALL CARDS

Bowman began issuing collectors' cards in 1949, the year the NBA was formed. The first set had 72 cards. These cards, about 2 inches square, were smaller than modern examples.

The cardboard press tags used to identify reporters covering basketball games are rare collectibles. The examples shown are from the National Collegiate Athletic Association tournaments of 1958, 1961, 1962 and 1963. They are worth $12 to $18 each.

These Topps basketball cards, made in 1969, are unusually long. Although the public didn't like the format, the cards are popular with collectors. These mementos cost 20 cents to 60 cents each.

Bowman's cards were not popular. Neither were cards issued by the Topps Chewing Gum Co., the leader in the field, in 1958.

**Topps Chewing Gum Co.**—Finally, in 1969, Topps tried again. This time the company issued odd-sized cards nearly 5 inches long and 2-1/2 inches wide. After establishing a market for basketball cards, Topps began marketing them in the traditional size. These cards are now enthusiastically collected.

**Fleer**—In 1961, Fleer, another chewing-gum manufacturer, produced a series of cards featuring 66 NBA players.

The tops from small ice-cream containers issued by Carvel in 1975 are also collectible. These feature such stars as Dave Cowens and Kareem Abdul-Jabbar.

## COLLECTING BASKETBALL MEMORABILIA

Basketball mementos became collectible more recently than baseball and football items. You can buy basketball memorabilia at garage sales, estate auctions, even church or benefit sales. The items you find will probably cost a fraction of what they will be worth someday.

Very few dealers handle basketball memorabilia. You can sometimes find basketball items in sports-autograph collections. You can sometimes locate paper items in ephemera dealers' files. Such dealers often have a sports category that includes numerous miscellaneous items.

If you want to collect equipment or uniforms, try advertising in sports publications. Ads in basketball *fanzines,* magazines devoted to the sport, sometimes produce surprising results.

Basketball mementos usually appear at auction only when a well-known player, club owner or avid fan dies. Sports magazines carry announcements about such auctions.

---

### BUYING AND SELLING BASKETBALL COLLECTIBLES

● Basketball cards are easy to find and inexpensive. Buy them now, while prices are low. These cards will increase in value as more enthusiasts enter the field.

● Jerseys, sweat shirts and jackets worn by important professional players are becoming popular. The most valuable are those worn by stars such as Jerry West and Wilt Chamberlain.

---

Sports Collectibles **23**

# ICE-HOCKEY COLLECTIBLES

Ice hockey developed from ice skating. It originated in Canada during the 1870s and later became popular in the United States. The rules of the modern game were established during the 1880s. In 1893, the Stanley Cup was first awarded for the Canadian amateur championship.

Today, ice hockey is one of America's favorite indoor spectator sports. The Stanley Cup has become the symbol of professional hockey supremacy. Ice hockey combines tradition with lively competition, and its fans are known for their enthusiasm.

Although ice hockey is played in several European countries, most collectors are interested only in American and Canadian hockey mementos. A few enthusiasts collect equipment and shoulder patches used by Russian and Swedish teams. The basic collecting categories are the same as those for other sports.

## ICE-HOCKEY EQUIPMENT

Jerseys, headgear, shoulder patches and complete uniforms are the most popular ice-hockey collectibles. A complete uniform worn by a well-known player costs $600 or more.

Enthusiasts also look for such items as goaltenders' pads, masks and gloves. Hockey sticks and pucks are also collectible, and are easily displayed.

Ice-hockey equipment, like that of most sports, often carries facsimile signatures. These add little value to a stick or glove. Real autographs are another matter. They can greatly increase the value of a piece.

## ICE-HOCKEY EPHEMERA

Ice-hockey programs, ticket stubs, posters and press guides are not popular with many collectors. Therefore, these items are readily available and inexpensive. As with other professional sports, ephemera related to league championships are the most popular.

Because college ice-hockey leagues are a recent development, collectors have not yet expressed much interest in buying memorabilia related to them. You might consider exploring this area while prices are low and items are easy to find.

## ICE-HOCKEY CARDS

The Topps Chewing Gum Co. has printed ice-hockey cards since 1954. These cards are inexpensive because they are relatively new and thousands are in circulation. A collector can easily acquire a complete set for each year from 1954 to the present.

Because Canadian players figure prominently in the game, several Canadian companies manufacture collectors' cards. One of the best-known is Parkhurst, which entered the field in 1951.

Collectors' cards featuring hockey players are inexpensive and easy to find. The most valuable examples show popular players, such as Glen "Chico" Resch of the New York Islanders. The cards shown here were made between 1968 and 1980. They cost 20 cents to 40 cents apiece.

## BUYING AND SELLING HOCKEY COLLECTIBLES

• Hockey cards offer great opportunities for beginning collectors. Because few people collect them, such cards are inexpensive. An extensive collection of these cards will increase in value. As with all collectors' cards, buy only examples in fine or mint condition.

• Clothing worn by a well-known player is also becoming popular. A jacket worn by a lesser-known player on a championship team is also collectible.

• Always try to get the history of any piece of equipment you buy. Who wore it and when? How did the seller acquire it? Such information is part of what antique dealers call the *provenance,* or history, of an object. The more interesting the history, the more valuable the item may be.

## COLLECTING ICE-HOCKEY MEMORABILIA

Although ice hockey is very popular, few collectors concentrate on mementos associated with the sport.

Very few dealers specialize in ice-hockey memorabilia. You can sometimes find items in general collections or in ephemera dealers' files.

Check garage sales, estate sales and secondhand stores. Because so few people are interested in ice-hockey memorabilia, you can sometimes find excellent bargains.

Your best bet is to advertise in ice-hockey fanzines. Such magazines also carry news of auctions of ice-hockey mementos. Members of collectors' clubs are also good sources for memorabilia.

# GOLF COLLECTIBLES

Golf originated in Scotland during the 15th century. During the 17th century, the Dutch inhabitants of New Amsterdam, known today as New York City, played golf. They made golf balls from deerskin and dug the holes in the village green. The Dutch were enthusiastic golfers, and their games frequently spread into the streets. The city's early records include numerous complaints of windows smashed by golf balls.

By the late 1880s the sport had become popular throughout the United States. Today, golf is arguably America's most popular "country-club" sport. Millions of people play the game and millions watch important matches on television.

Most collectible golf mementos were made during the 1880s or later. Because few collectors are interested in these items, prices are low. You can assemble a comprehensive collection inexpensively. Major collecting categories include equipment, ephemera and trophies.

### GOLF EQUIPMENT

Iron or iron-and-wood golf clubs are the most popular mementos. The Spalding Golf Museum in Dundee, Scotland, has an iron club made in 1680 by Robert Clark, one of the first golf-club manufacturers.

No American golf clubs date back to that period. In fact, 18th-century American clubs are difficult to find, even though many types were produced.

The design of golf clubs and the materials from which they are made have changed continually over the years. Shafts, which originally were wood, are now steel, graphite or titanium. This evolution means enthusiasts can choose among numerous types of collectible clubs.

Today we refer to golf clubs by numbers. However, clubs once had names. One 19th-century source describes *drivers, brassies,* and *spoons*. These are now called *No. 1, No. 2* and *No. 3 woods*.

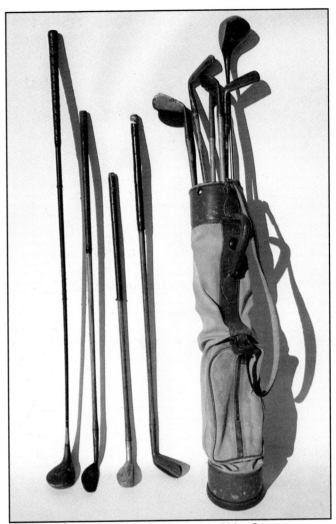

Early golf clubs include a brass-headed MacGregor putter, $100 to $125, and a Jack Gordon Special Putter, $70 to $85. The golf bag, made between 1915 and 1925, is worth $50 to $65. Early golf clubs and bags are popular with collectors. Look for clubs with wood, rather than steel, shafts. Many clubs made between 1910 and 1920 cost $25 to $40 each.

As with other sports equipment, enthusiasts often collect by manufacturer or time period. Look for left-handed sets. They are rarer than right-handed sets.

Golf balls have also gone through many changes and are popular collectibles.

Enthusiasts also buy golf tees. Early wood examples and later aluminum and plastic models are the most popular.

Golf bags, turf repairers, stymie markers and green's-level gauges are also popular collectibles. You can find examples of the last three items in sterling silver.

### GOLF EPHEMERA

Paper goods associated with golf include programs from famous tournaments, score cards, players' autographs and posters advertising major events. Numerous how-to and historical books are also available.

## GOLF TROPHIES

Most trophies were awarded to winners of obscure tournaments. Even so, these trophies are attractive mementos.

Most trophies are made of electroplated silver. A few sterling-silver examples are also available. The largest manufacturer, the Dodge Trophy Co. of Crystal Lake, Illinois, produces thousands of trophies each year.

If you want to collect trophies, don't hesitate to buy examples that have lost much of their silver plating. Such mementos are usually inexpensive and can be replated at moderate cost.

## COLLECTING GOLF MEMORABILIA

One way players try to improve their game is by purchasing new clubs. As a result, attics and storerooms are crammed with discarded clubs. Garage sales and flea markets are good sources for old equipment.

Many antique dealers stock old golf clubs. Second-hand shops and junk dealers also have golf equipment.

You can find trophies in many places, including flea markets. You can buy paper goods from ephemera dealers.

If you decide to collect golf memorabilia, you will have little competition. The more you learn about this category, the more excellent bargains you will find.

---

### BUYING AND SELLING GOLF COLLECTIBLES

• Golf clubs are often stored in an attic until someone throws them away during spring cleaning. You may be able to "rescue" a set of nice clubs at a garage sale.
• Advertise in your local newspaper. Make your ads clear and concise. Tell people exactly what you want.
• Golf clubs usually cost $5 to $20 each. Don't pay more unless you know the piece is very old or rare.

---

Novelty items associated with golf could be an individual collecting category. Shown here are a pot-metal cigarette box, $20 to $25; ceramic salt-and-pepper shakers shaped like golf balls, $15 to $20 a pair; and a bronzed pot-metal ashtray with the figure of a golfer, $35 to $45. All were made between 1935 and 1955.

Early golf balls are very rare. These date from 1890 to 1910 and are worth $45 to $55 each. The cardboard periscope made for the U.S. Open is $30 to $35. The ceramic bookends featuring golfers cost $20 to $25. The bound copy of the 1965 *Golf Digest* sells for $35 to $45.

# TENNIS COLLECTIBLES

Tennis is a popular participation and spectator sport. Millions of tennis fans follow the careers of the game's superstars. However, tennis has not yet attracted great collector interest. Therefore, it is an excellent area for beginning collectors and those of modest means.

The modern version of tennis was created in 1873 by an Englishman, Major Walter C. Wingfield. He combined elements of court tennis, racquets and badminton.

Tennis was first played at a garden party in Wales. A year later, in 1874, an American named Mary Ewing Outerbridge saw the game being played in Bermuda. She took rackets, balls and a net back to her home in Staten Island, New York, and built the first court there. The game quickly spread across the country. Popularity has increased steadily since the 1940s.

The major collecting categories for tennis include equipment, ephemera and trophies.

## TENNIS EQUIPMENT

The most treasured tennis memento is the racket. Rackets that have been owned or autographed by well-known players are especially prized. The autograph of someone such as Don Budge or Pancho Gonzalez significantly increases a racket's value. Make sure a signature is a genuine autograph, not a facsimile added by manufacturers. Facsimiles do not affect value.

Early tennis rackets were basically square and had a small hitting surface. They were made of wood strung with animal fiber called *catgut*. This term has never been popular because many people believe it refers to cats' intestines. It does not. Although catgut is made from animals' intestines, cats' intestines are never used.

Most collectors' attention has focused on early wood rackets. A few wise collectors are looking for early metal, fiberglass and graphite rackets. These more modern rackets will soon be very valuable.

Wood presses or clamps used to keep rackets from warping are also collectible. Other items to look for include sun visors, early tennis shoes and balls. White balls, once standard, have vanished from courts during the past decade.

An interesting collection could be built around the canvas covers used to protect rackets. These could easily be displayed on a wall.

Tennis-racket prices depend on age and rarity. These examples include traditional wood rackets and an early metal racket. They were made between 1920 and 1960, and are worth $20 to $50 each.

Early tennis rackets were shaped and glued in this mold. It dates from the early 1900s and is worth $400 to $550.

## TENNIS EPHEMERA

Because tennis has been a popular spectator sport only since the late 1940s, most tennis ephemera is of fairly recent vintage. Programs from famous matches, posters, autographs, and books and magazines about tennis are collectible.

Magazine covers showing future stars are especially valuable. Tracy Austin appeared on the cover of *World Tennis* when she was only 4 years old!

## TENNIS TROPHIES

Sterling-silver or silver-plated trophies commemorating major matches of the past half-century are difficult to find. Most are in private collections or museums. Look for trophies awarded to winners of local contests. Concentrate on the sculptural quality of the trophy. If it is well-designed, it becomes a sculpture, not just a tennis memento.

## COLLECTING TENNIS MEMORABILIA

Tennis rackets have evolved over the past four decades. Their size, shape and materials have changed. Most players discard old rackets for newer models. For this reason, tennis rackets often can be found at garage sales.

Some antique dealers stock tennis memorabilia. Early rackets are becoming especially popular, and dealers frequently have several.

You can also find trophies at garage sales and antique shops.

Ephemera dealers often carry tennis-related items. Remember that most ephemera dealers display only a fraction of their wares. If you don't see what you want, ask.

Secondhand shops and junk dealers sometimes carry tennis equipment. Rackets are usually easy to find. Buy old rackets now. As tennis becomes more popular with collectors, prices will increase.

---

### BUYING AND SELLING TENNIS COLLECTIBLES

- You can often find tennis rackets at garage sales and in secondhand stores. Advertising in local papers can also bring good results.
- Remember that old rackets are subject to warping and dry rot.
- If you want to restore a racket's strings, use catgut. It costs more than nylon, but nylon is not appropriate for a 1920s racket.
- Tennis rackets usually cost $15 to $35 each. Rare or interesting rackets cost more.

---

These interesting go-withs were made during the 1920s. They include a racket press, $15 to $35; racket case, $30 to $45; and canvas racket cover, $30 to $40.

Bronze sculptures of tennis players can cost $250 to $1,000, or much less, depending on the sculptor's fame. This piece, made between 1900 and 1910, is worth $35 to $50.

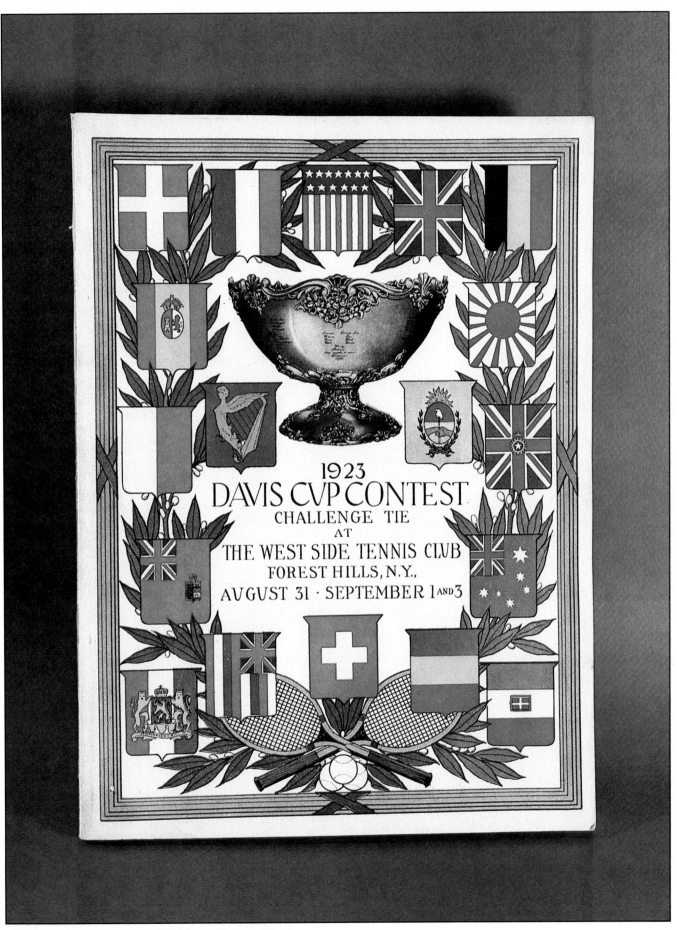

This is the program for the 1923 Davis Cup match at Forest Hills, New York. It is especially valuable because Bill Tilden was on the U.S. team. Such programs have become popular collectibles. This example costs $60 to $80.

# FISHING COLLECTIBLES

Fishing has long been an important part of American life. George Washington was a fisherman. You can see his equipment on display at his Mount Vernon home.

It was not until this century that people began collecting old fishing tackle as a hobby. This sport offers several collecting categories. Each provides interesting opportunities.

## FISHING RODS

There are several types of fishing rods. All are collectible.

**Fly Rods**—The most expensive fly rods are those used in trout and salmon fishing. Until the 1860s, these long, delicate tools were made of ash, maple or hickory. Then Asian bamboo, or *cane,* was introduced. In this century, metal and fiberglass have dominated the field. Most enthusiasts prefer rods made from the older materials.

Fly rods can be expensive. Early examples are especially costly. Fly rods by H. L. Leonard or William Mitchell, who were working before 1880, cost about $1,000.

Factory-made rods produced between 1920 and 1950 are less expensive. These rods were made by such

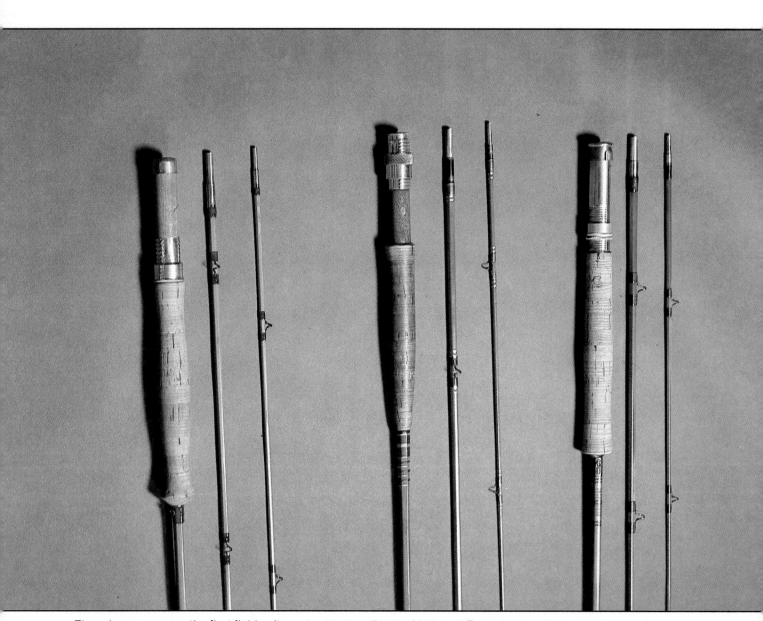

Fly rods were among the first fishing items to attract collectors' interest. Early, hard-to-find examples such as these are expensive. From left to right: Payne, 8-1/2 feet long, $550 to $600; Equinox, The Orvis Co. Inc., Manchester, Vermont, 8-1/2 feet long, $250 to $300; Model 49DF, H. L. Leonard Co., Bangor, Maine, 7-1/2 feet long, $475 to $550. These fly rods are split bamboo and were made between 1910 and 1945.

large sporting-goods manufacturers as South Bend Tackle Co., South Bend, Indiana; Wright & McGill, Abbey & Imbrie, and Montague City Rod and Reel Co., Brooklyn, New York.

**Casting Rods—**The short, stiff rods used in bait casting were originally made of wood. Later examples are steel and fiberglass. Casting rods are usually less expensive than fly rods. However, a 19th-century example made of thin pieces of ash glued together is worth several hundred dollars.

Saltwater rods are more reasonably priced. These include short, thick boat rods and the longer surf-casting rods. Because few collectors are exploring this field, you can find some excellent bargains.

Spin-casting did not become popular in the United States until the mid-1940s. Because spin-casting rods are fairly new, they are inexpensive.

Early fly reels can be very expensive. Clockwise from top: The Orvis reel, complete with wood case, was patented in 1874. It is a bargain at $300 to $350. The tiny H. L. Leonard Co. reel was patented in 1877 and is worth $900 to $1,000. The rare aluminum reel, by England's Hardy Bros., costs $900 to $1,100. The silver-and-black Perfection trout reel, by Edward and Julius Vom Hofe, New York City and Brooklyn, New York, is valued at $700 to $800.

These fly reels are reasonably priced. Left: Vernley, Horrocks-Ibbotson Co., Utica, New York, made of Bakelite, $25 to $35. Right: Rainbow, A. F. Meisselbach Bros. Newark, New Jersey, $40 to $55. Both were made between 1930 and 1940.

Remember that the rod's value depends partly on its manufacturer. Fortunately, about 80% of all rods are marked by their manufacturers.

On some rods, the manufacturer's name is stenciled on the rod itself. On others, the name is stamped into the metal base, or *pocket cap,* at the end of the handle.

Beginning collectors should learn the names of important early manufacturers. Remember that major manufacturers, such as James Heddon & Sons,

Used primarily for fly and bait fishing, wood reels have a great handcrafted look. They are a favorite with decorators. Left to right: Reel with brass fittings, $150 to $200; reel with silver plate, dated 1890, $250 to $300; unusually small example, $50 to $60; reel with ebony handles, $120 to $150. These date from 1880 to 1910.

Dowagiac, Michigan; William Shakespeare Jr. Co., Kalamazoo, Michigan; and the South Bend Tackle Co., made all types of rods. You could build a large collection of the products of any of these firms.

## FISHING REELS

Many types of reels are available.

**Fly Reels**—Fly reels, used with fly rods, are usually *single-action*. Each time you turn the handle, the spool revolves once. These reels are designed primarily to hold the fishing line. Some have solid sides. Others have perforated sides, which reduce the weight of the reel and provide ventilation to dry the line.

Automatic fly reels are also available. When you pull these, a triggerlike device causes the line to run in without reeling.

Most fly reels are 2-1/2 inches to 3-1/2 inches in diameter. Larger examples, up to 6 inches across, were used in salmon fishing.

Fly reels have been made in this country since the early 19th century. Examples marked by famous early manufacturers, such as Edward and Julius Vom Hofe, of New York City and Brooklyn, New York; A. F. Meisselbach & Bros., Newark, New Jersey; and The Orvis Co. Inc., Manchester, Vermont, cost hundreds of dollars. Manufacturers' names and patent dates are usually stamped into the sides or base of the reel.

Fly reels were made of brass, nickel-plated brass, aluminum, hard rubber, even wood.

**Casting Reels**—Casting reels were nearly always made of metal. These heavier mechanisms are designed to cast a heavy lure. The lure is then reeled in to simulate the movement of live bait.

Casting reels appeared during the 1830s. The most famous are the *Kentucky reels* made by such firms as J. F. & B. F. Meek of Frankfort, Kentucky. These are museum pieces. They cost as much as $1,000 when they come on the market. Later casting reels, by firms such as Pflueger Enterprises Manufacturing Co., Akron, Ohio; South Bend Tackle Co., Ocean City, often cost less than $50.

Most casting reels are *multiplying reels*. When you turn the handle once, the spool turns two, three or four times. Multiplying reels draw in the line much faster than other types.

**Saltwater Reels**—Saltwater reels range from oversized casting reels to heavy, single-action boat reels designed for fighting large fish. These reels are becoming popular with collectors.

**Spinning Reels**—These reels have been ignored by collectors. They will become more popular in the future.

## CASTING LURES

Casting rods and reels are designed to throw out and then pull back several types of bait, or *lures*. These

Although few collectors are interested in trout flies, knowledgeable enthusiasts pay large sums for examples made by famous fly-tiers. These dry flies, made between 1950 and 1960, cost $1 to $2 each.

Fishermen use bamboo, rush or willow creels to store the day's catch. This example dates from 1920 to 1940 and costs $15 to $35. Look for rare wood or metal creels and for those with the fish hole in the center of the lid instead of on the side.

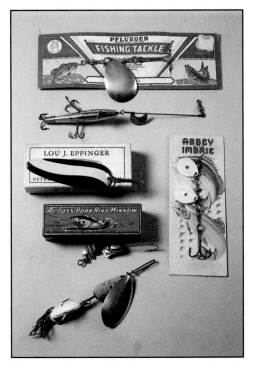

Many casting and trolling spoons and spinners are available. Some examples shown here have their original cards or boxes, which increases their value. Clockwise from the top: Colorado Spinner, Pflueger Enterprises Manufacturing Co., Akron, Ohio, $2 to $5; Breakless Devon Minnow, Pflueger $15 to $25; Abbey & Imbrie spinner, $12 to $15; Brush Floating Spoon, patented in 1876, $75 to $100; Al Foss Pork Rind Minnow, $10 to $17; Eppinger Daredevil, $2 to $5.

Paintings of fishing scenes are valuable. This original oil painting of a catch of brook trout from New York's Adirondack Mountains was painted in 1905 and is worth $400 to $600. Examples by well-known artists cost thousands of dollars.

wood, metal or plastic baits resemble, in movement or appearance, fish, frogs or other small creatures.

**Spoons, Spinners, Plugs**—Baits include spoons, spinners and plugs.

Spoons and spinners are metal. They first appeared in the mid-19th century. Spoons are egg-shaped and wobble as they are pulled through the water. Spinners consist of propeller-shaped bits of metal mounted on a shaft. They spin as they are pulled back through the water. The most famous early manufacturer of spoons and spinners was J. T. Buel. A Buel spoon is very valuable.

Early plugs were fish-shaped objects made of carved, painted wood. They had metal fins, propellers and devices to make them sink or wobble. Plugs first appeared in 1887. They were most popular between 1900 and 1941.

After World War II, the bodies of plugs were usually made of plastic instead of wood.

Spinners, spoons and plugs are all equipped with one or more sets of barbed treble hooks.

Some people collect spoons and spinners, but many enthusiasts have acquired casting plugs during the past five years. Casting plugs are popular for several reasons. Even though most were made in factories, they have an appealing, almost folk-art appearance. They also have charming names, such as Glo-Lite Mouse, Pikie Minnow or River Runt. Collectors also like casting plugs because they can acquire a complete set by a single manufacturer.

Although they are popular, many examples are available for $10 or less. Important names to look for include Heddon, Arbogast, True Temper, Creek Chub and Paw Paw. Names are imprinted on the lures or on the boxes in which they are packed.

**Boxes**—Boxes are important. If you buy a lure in its original box, don't throw the box away. The box doubles the value of the lure! Other *go-withs,* such as instructional material, are also valuable.

## FISHING FLIES

Although called *flies,* these bits of feather, floss and tinsel are designed to resemble everything from bugs to minnows. They are used to lure trout, salmon, bass and dozens of saltwater species. They have not proven quite so successful at luring collectors, however.

Assembling an extensive, documented fishing-fly collection is difficult. Flies are usually small. They are not marked. You must try to determine the manufacturer by the history of the fly or by its resemblance to other items made by a known company or fly tier. Flies are also susceptible to damage from insects, especially moths. Even so, collectors will pay up to $100 for a desirable fly. Most collections are mounted behind glass or are kept in mothproof cabinets.

## MISCELLANEOUS FISHING EQUIPMENT

Fishermen use a great deal of equipment, or *tackle*. Such equipment includes storage boxes, nets, bamboo or canvas creels, fly books and lure cases. All are collectible.

Brightly colored cork-and-wood bobbers are very popular. Bobbers are used to float bait over fish. *Tip ups* used for ice fishing are also valuable. These devices send up a flag when a fish takes the bait.

## BOOKS AND PERIODICALS

Numerous fishing books are available. The best-known is Izaak Walton's *The Compleat Angler*. First published in 1653, this book is still popular today and is available in modern, updated editions.

The best-known American books are Ray Bergman's *Just Fishing* and James A. Henshall's *The Book of the Black Bass*. Both are classics, and early editions bring high prices.

Several fishing and hunting magazines are collectible. Some magazines have been published since the 19th century. Collectors usually attempt to obtain complete runs covering several years of one publication. Copies of *Field and Stream, Hunting and Fishing* and *Rod and Gun* are easy to find.

Fishing-tackle catalogs issued by manufacturers and retailers are also popular. The first appeared in 1839. These contain a wealth of information about old tackle. They also have extremely attractive illustrations.

## PAINTINGS, PRINTS AND TROPHIES

Fishermen like to have a memento of a successful

Calendar art is very collectible. This lithograph was an advertisement for the products of the Horton Manufacturing Co., Bristol, Conn., maker of Bristol Steel fishing rods. It is valued at $250 to $300.

day. In earlier times, such mementos included paintings of a hooked trout or leaping tarpon. For those who could not afford an original painting, there were prints. The famous lithographers Currier & Ives produced several attractive fishing scenes.

For fishermen who wanted an even more realistic memento there was taxidermy. An amazing number of "stuffed" fish and "stuffed" fish heads have survived. Proud owners display these trophies as proof of their expertise. Such trophies provide status for their owners—even if someone else caught the fish!

Few enthusiasts confine themselves to collecting fishing prints and trophies. However, such items are excellent additions to a collection of rods, reels or lures.

## COLLECTING FISHING MEMORABILIA

Fishing collectibles have become so popular that many antique dealers stock a few early rods or reels. Some dealers specialize in fishing collectibles. Such items occasionally come up at auction.

One of the best ways to find collectibles is to contact older fishermen or their families. Talking with members of local fish-and-game clubs is also helpful.

Be sure to advertise in local newspapers. Few fishermen throw away tackle. They just put it in an attic or cellar until a relative or persevering collector asks about it.

You can also locate memorabilia through collectors' clubs. Members are usually eager to swap or buy lures and other tackle.

When you buy mementos, don't ignore items made after 1950. Such items will increase in value as earlier pieces become harder to find and more expensive.

---

### BUYING AND SELLING FISHING COLLECTIBLES

● If you collect rods and reels, remember that condition is very important. Damaged or extensively restored examples are worth much less than examples in good original condition.

● Look for important manufacturers' names, such as Vom Hofe, Orvis and South Bend.

● If you want to explore a new area, try spinning rods, reels and lures. Most American-made examples were produced after 1945. Few collectors have shown much interest in this field.

● If you are interested in calendars, catalogs and trade journals, check old barns and sheds. Such publications were often nailed to the walls of such structures or were stored in them. You can sometimes find catalogs in old fishing-tackle boxes.

● Don't forget "stuffed" trophy fish that have been treated by a taxidermist. Even if you didn't catch the big ones, you can still collect them. Avoid damaged examples. They are expensive to repair.

# HUNTING COLLECTIBLES

Thousands of American men and women enjoy hunting. One reason the sport is popular is that it has always been a democratic activity. From the founding of our country, hunting has been open to young and old, rich and poor.

This was seldom the case in other parts of the world, where the right to own guns and hunt was often reserved for the rich and privileged. Less than 200 years ago, wealthy European landowners protected their estates from poachers by using *man traps*. These devices were designed to seriously injure trespassers.

European nobility often hunted with packs of dogs and hundreds of *beaters,* who tramped through the woods stirring up game. Hunters in the United States pursued a more individual sport. When Americans think of hunting, they think of James Fenimore Cooper's Hawkeye with his trusty long rifle. Or they think of buffalo hunters with their powerful Sharps or Henry rifles, weapons referred to as *buffalo guns.*

Today, such firearms are among the most popular hunting memorabilia. Guns are only one type of collectible, however. The major collecting categories include sporting firearms; gunning equipment; cartridges, shells and loading materials; ephemera; and trophies.

## SPORTING FIREARMS

An astonishing number of firearms are available. Rifles, shotguns and handguns come in all shapes and sizes. One reason why is that they have been made for a long time.

Firearms became widely used in the 16th century. Since then, thousands of different types have been produced. At first, most firearms were designed for warfare and hunting. However, within a short period of time, highly specialized weapons designed only for hunting appeared. Today, many types of *sporting firearms* exist. Collectors usually specialize in one type.

**Long Guns**—Several distinctions are made among sporting firearms. The first is between *long guns* and *handguns*. Long guns have long barrels and are used in hunting. Handguns have barrels less than eight inches long. Some handguns are used in hunting, but most col-

This Kentucky rifle was made by gunsmith Joseph Golcher. Like most such weapons, it was actually produced in Pennsylvania. These rifles were made between 1750 and 1850 and are worth $1,000 to $3,500. The stamped-brass powder flask dates from 1870 to 1880 and costs $50 to $75.

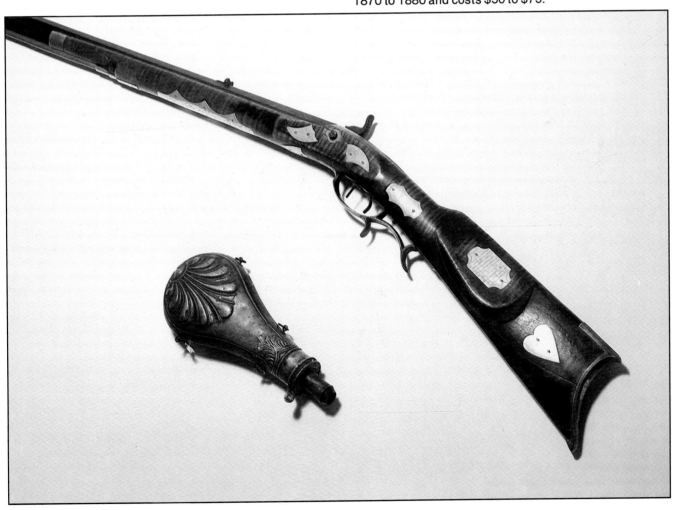

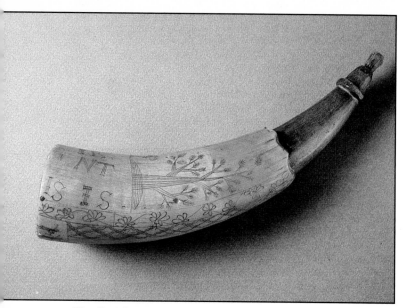

The first American powder horns were carved from cow horns. Scratch-carved decoration greatly enhances the value. This example was made in Connecticut between 1800 and 1850. It costs $750 to $900. Undecorated examples are worth $20 to $65.

lectors are interested primarily in long guns.

Long guns include rifles and shotguns. These guns are either muzzle-loading or breech-loading. Muzzle-loading firearms are loaded through the muzzle. Breech-loading weapons are loaded behind the barrel.

Further distinctions exist among early firearms. The most important is the way in which a weapon is fired. As firing mechanisms were improved, previous weapons became obsolete. Matchlocks gave way to wheel locks, which in turn were replaced by flintlocks. The percussion cap was invented about 1850. This was a small paper or metal container that held a charge and exploded when struck. Collectors are especially interested in percussion-cap firearms, many of which are still available.

Because sporting firearms are so specialized, you may want to confine your collection to one type. For example, you could collect rifles or shotguns designed for specific game. You could buy bird or wildfowl guns, small game rifles, or rifles designed for big game, such as bears or elephants.

**Kentucky Rifles**—Because of their close association with American history, some firearms are especially prized by American collectors. The best-known are the *Kentucky rifles,* most of which were made in Pennsylvania! These long-barreled weapons were made from about 1750 to 1850. They were usually beautifully decorated and very accurate.

The value of any sporting firearm depends greatly on its markings. Most rifles and shotguns were marked with the name and sometimes the address of the manufacturer. The name of a famous manufacturer can increase a weapon's value by thousands of dollars. Kentucky rifles have sold for as much as $20,000.

**Plains Rifles**—The *Plains rifle* is similar to the Kentucky rifle. Both have the same basic design and firing mechanism. However, the Plains rifle has a short barrel and could be handled easily from horseback. Some years ago a Plains rifle owned by the legendary Kit Carson was sold at auction for thousands of dollars. Any weapon owned by a famous person is usually very valuable.

**Famous Manufacturers**—Most collectors can't afford to buy Kentucky rifles or 19th-century, .55-caliber elephant guns. But many weapons made between 1880 and 1960 are reasonably priced. Look for the names of famous and popular manufacturers. These include Winchester, Remington, Savage, Mossberg, Ithaca, Browning, Iver Johnson, Marlin, and H & R. These firms produced thousands of examples of different types of guns. These weapons are readily available and cost $75 or more. Early octagonal-barrel .22-caliber *plinkers* used for small game and target shooting are especially good investments.

The prices of sporting firearms vary widely. Some "old looking" 19th-century flintlocks are worth $100 or less. Rare or customized rifles and shotguns from the 1940s and 1950s cost thousands of dollars. Age is not always the most important factor. You must learn about firearms to invest wisely. If you read gun books and examine gun collections, you may find a real prize!

You could also assemble an interesting collection of unusual weapons. These include such oddities as three- or four-barreled guns, and weapons combining the characteristics of a rifle and a shotgun. Many such firearms are available. Although they weren't necessarily practical for hunting, they are wonderful conversation pieces.

## GUNNING EQUIPMENT

Hunters require a great deal of equipment. These items, called *gunning equipment,* are collectible. Perhaps the most interesting mementos are the *powder horns* used to carry black powder in the days before cartridges.

**Powder Horns**—The first powder horns were aptly named. They were made of hollow cow horn plugged at each end with a piece of wood. Although homemade, powder horns are surprisingly easy to find and inexpensive.

Some powder horns were decorated, usually by their owners. Such items are rare and expensive. The decorations include maps, drawings, and the owners' names. Powder horns made during the Revolutionary War are worth $10,000. But don't be fooled by fakes!

Brass or copper flask-shaped powder horns made during the 19th century are also valuable. They were produced in factories and often have a manufacturer's mark. Look for flasks with embossed decorations.

The bright colors and appealing graphics of the boxes in which shotgun shells were packed make such items a growing favorite with collectors. These examples, by Winchester Group, East Alton, Ill., Remington Arms Co., Bridgeport, Conn., and Peters are worth $25 to $50 each. They were made between 1930 and 1940. Boxes are more valuable if they contain original shells.

Catalogs produced by manufacturers of sporting firearms and ammunition are very popular. Clockwise, from upper left: Lyman gun sights catalog, 1892, $30 to $35; Marlin Fire Arms catalog, 1899, $70 to $85; edition of *Colt on the Trail,* 1934, $20 to $25; Parker Guns catalog, 1932, $35 to $50.

**Hunting Knives**—These weapons are important collectibles. Most knives were used to skin and cut up dead game. However, the famous *Bowie Knife,* which was 18 inches long, was sometimes used to kill buffalo from horseback. Occasionally referred to as *Arkansas toothpicks,* Bowie knives are hard to find and expensive.

Many hunting and utility knives are available. Look for marks by manufacturers such as Camillus Cutlery of Camillus, New York; Barlow; J. Russel & Co. of Green River, Pennsylvania; Waldeman; and Remington. Most have steel blades and steel or hardwood handles. Some have handles made of stag horn, ivory, ebony or brass. Handles made of these materials add interest and value to hunting knives.

**Gun Cases and Cabinets**—A well-made gun cabinet or rack can bring a substantial price. Gun racks made from deer antlers or other horns are especially valuable.

**Cleaning Tools**—Cleaning rods and other tools used to maintain or repair guns are collectible. Game bags, gun straps and the pouches in which equipment is carried also interest enthusiasts.

Some collectors buy hunting clothes. Most clothing and boots are reasonably priced. Exceptions include articles made of sheepskin, deerskin or other exotic materials, and items owned by a famous hunter.

## CARTRIDGES, SHELLS AND LOADING MATERIALS

If you lack the space or money to collect guns, you may enjoy the growing field of ammunition collecting. Thousands of different types of ammunition in various calibers have been produced during the last 200 years. Some rare examples cost as much as $400, but these are exceptions. Most cartridges and shotgun shells cost 50 cents to $1 each.

**Cartridges**—These items consist of a bullet, powder and primer, all enclosed in a metal case. They are used in rifles and handguns. The term *shot shell* applies to shotgun ammunition, which is usually enclosed in a paper or plastic skin. Both types were made by the same firms that produced the guns in which the ammunition was used.

**Ammunition Boxes**—The cardboard boxes in which ammunition was sold are interesting collectibles. A box's value depends on the age and rarity of the product it contained.

Federal Migratory Bird Hunting Stamps were first collected by stamp enthusiasts but are now popular with hunters. Most duck stamps, including those shown here, sell for $5 to $8 each in used condition. Used stamps bear the signature of a hunter. Note the unsigned 1971 stamp. It is worth $25 to $30. Unsigned stamps bring premium prices.

The Labrador Retriever

Hunting prints can be very valuable, especially those made in limited editions by important artists. If you want a nice print for a modest sum, look for mass-produced examples. The one shown here is worth $30 to $40.

**Bullets**—Before the development of cartridges, guns were hand-loaded. Bullets were often made at home. Relics of those days are collectible. Look for bullet molds, loading tools, powder measures and the tin cans in which black powder was sold.

As with cartridge boxes, the value of powder cans is partly based on the beauty of the decoration.

## HUNTING EPHEMERA

Many interesting types of paper goods are associated with hunting. Catalogs issued by gun and ammunition manufacturers are especially prized. Catalogs printed by such firms as Winchester and Remington during the 19th century are hard to find and expensive. Damaged examples have only a fraction of the value of catalogs in good condition.

**Posters, Calendars, Ads**—Posters and calendars with hunting scenes interest some enthusiasts. Advertisements for firearms are also collectible. Produced in great quantity during the past century, these items range in value from a few dollars to $1,500. Those with the signatures of well-known poster artists are especially valuable. Such artists include Edmund Osthaus, Lynn Bogue Hunt and Phillip R. Goodwin.

**Duck Stamps**—Federal and state *duck stamps* are interesting collectibles. These licensing stamps are issued to hunters for a fee. The federal government has issued duck stamps since 1934. Twenty states also issue such stamps.

The typical duck stamp is printed in color and shows one or more ducks in a natural setting. The rarest federal example is the 1935 issue. It costs as much as $200. State duck stamps are often harder to find and more expensive. Some cost nearly $1,000.

One appeal of collecting ammunition or duck stamps is that they present few storage or display problems. The same is true of hunting badges.

**Hunting Badges**—From early in this century until after World War II, hunting badges were issued to licensed hunters for identification. Most badges were celluloid and metal. They carry a number, the year and the name of the issuing state. Most collectors buy examples from a single state or region. These collectibles are very inexpensive.

**Hunting Licenses**—Modern·printed hunting licenses are a relatively unexplored collecting field. These licenses are designed to be carried in a wallet or worn on a jacket or cap. As with fishing licenses, these licenses contain information about the owner. Some are illustrated with hunting scenes. Because few people collect hunting licenses, they are very inexpensive.

## GAME TROPHIES

Until recently, many wealthy, well-traveled hunters collected game trophies. Such trophies included antlers or horns, skins, heads, even entire bodies. The trophies are preserved through the art of taxidermy. Today, popular taste and the laws governing the taking and display of animals have changed. Most hunters are content with a modest deer rack or two. Federal law prohibits the ownership of trophies from many endangered species.

Many collectors are interested in game trophies. Impressive racks of deer antlers, moose heads, elk horns and bearskins cost hundreds of dollars. Enthusiasts also buy pheasants, grouse and other game birds. Aficionados of sports memorabilia are not the only ones who collect these trophies. Many people use them to decorate walls.

## COLLECTING HUNTING MEMORABILIA

Hunting memorabilia presents the enthusiast with safety and legal concerns.

**Safety Considerations**—Guns and knives are dangerous. They should always be kept where they cannot be reached by children or adults who don't know how to use them.

Handle antique ammunition carefully. It often contains gunpowder.

**Legal Considerations**—Many states and municipalities have laws stating that only licensed individuals can own working firearms. The scope of these laws varies greatly. For example, New York City's gun-control law is much stricter than the laws in other areas of the state. Check the laws in your area before buying firearms.

Some states and municipalities also have laws concerning ownership of edged weapons, such as hunting knives. In most areas, it is not unlawful to own them, only to carry them in public. Consult local authorities about your rights and responsibilities.

**Federal Endangered Species Act**—Another important consideration is the Federal Endangered Species Act of 1973. This makes it illegal to buy or sell numerous animals and birds in interstate commerce. Included are owls, hawks and other birds not usually thought of as game. Before you buy a trophy, make sure the owner can legally sell it and that you can legally buy it.

**Where to Look**—You can find many items, such as old guns, hunting equipment, posters and calendars, at yard sales, auctions and secondhand shops. Prices are usually low.

High-quality firearms, such as Kentucky rifles, are usually sold only at auction, or by collectors or specialized dealers.

Hunting memorabilia is a field in which opportunities and prices vary. Familiarize yourself by talking with other collectors and reading publications related to your specialty.

Some trophy collectors concentrate on exotic foreign species. Others prefer American examples, such as the large deer skull and two smaller sets of horns shown here. The large trophy is worth $150 to $250. The smaller examples cost $30 to $40 each.

# BUYING AND SELLING
## HUNTING COLLECTIBLES

• The condition of an old gun affects its price. You should do restoration work only if you are an expert. Early weapons are dangerous. Barrels can explode. Projectiles can lodge in the breech or barrel. Fire these weapons only under proper test conditions.

• Some guns are very valuable, but most pre-1910 examples are not. A gun is not valuable just because it is old.

• With guns and most hunting memorabilia, the manufacturer's name is important. Always look for a manufacturer's mark. Never discard a carton or carrying case. These might be valuable. Items such as cartridge boxes and powder cans are also collectible.

• Gun-club journals and hunting and fishing magazines are good places to advertise for hunting memorabilia.

# DUCK AND SHORE-BIRD DECOYS

If you want to collect something truly American, try duck and shore-bird decoys.

Decoys are designed to lure prey close enough for hunters to get a good shot. They look like live birds and are small works of art.

When the first settlers arrived in this country from Europe, they found Native Americans using decoys. The Native Americans fashioned their decoys from rushes covered with skins or feathers. The new settlers began making their own decoys. They carved them from wood and painted them in the colors of the birds they hunted. During the late 19th century, a few factories made mass-produced decoys. However, many decoys are hand-carved even today.

Decoys attract collectors as well as game. Some collectors are hunters who treasure old decoys. Other enthusiasts buy decoys as folk art. They look for extremely well-carved examples and treat them as sculpture.

To compete with these knowledgeable enthusiasts, you need to learn about decoys. The two major types are *duck decoys* and *shore-bird decoys*.

## DUCK DECOYS

Many duck decoys look like migratory waterfowl. These ducks spend part of the year in warm southern climes and the remainder in northern areas. Most such ducks prefer freshwater ponds, lakes and streams, and the calm bays adjacent to large bodies of salt water. Ducks include blacks, mallards, pintails and canvasbacks.

**Sea-Duck Decoys**—Some decoys look like sea ducks. These waterfowl prefer the rougher salt waters of sounds, open bays and the ocean. Such sea ducks include the eider, merganser and scoter.

Sea-duck decoys are usually larger and heavier than other duck decoys. Their large size makes them more visible in rough, open waters.

Some decoys representing other types of waterfowl, such as Canada geese, swans or gulls, are also included in the duck-decoy category.

Large seagoing decoys such as this Maine eider have a strong sculptural quality that some collectors prize. This piece, made between 1920 and 1930 by an unknown carver, costs $250 to $400.

These factory-made shore-bird decoys are made of painted tin. A sanderling is in the foreground, a black-bellied plover is in the background. These decoys, in excellent condition, were made by an early manufacturer, Strater & Sohier, Boston. They are worth $150 to $250 each. Later examples and decoys that are damaged or have lost paint cost $35 to $85.

**Confidence Decoys**—Neither swans nor gulls are hunted. Hunters use decoys of these waterfowl as *confidence decoys*. The idea is that ducks seeing them floating on a body of water will think it is safe to land.

Swan, crane and heron decoys are very valuable. Folk-art collectors prize them for their large size and unusual shapes.

## SHORE-BIRD DECOYS

These decoys look like the long-legged birds that flit along saltwater beaches. Unlike duck decoys, shore-bird decoys do not float. They are fitted with a long stick, or *leg*, that is stuck in the sand or mud. These decoys are also called *stickup decoys*.

Some goose decoys are also made this way. Geese feed in open fields. Goose stickups usually have three legs rather than one.

Shore-bird decoys look like several kinds of birds, including sanderlings, plovers, curlews, yellowlegs and sandpipers. These birds are affectionately known as *peeps*. The sandpiper, only a few inches long, is the smallest of these birds. The curlew, about 19 inches long, is the largest.

By 1915, hunters had killed so many shore birds that the government intervened. Federal and state legislation prohibited the hunting of peeps. For this reason, most shore-bird decoys made after 1920 are fakes or display pieces.

## HOW DECOYS ARE MADE

Most duck decoys are carved from wood, usually

cedar or pine. The head is usually shaped separately and then set into the body with a dowel. Skilled carvers add the wings, tail and feathers.

Most decoys are painted to resemble real birds. Many decoys have painted eyes or eyes made of nailheads. Some duck and shore-bird decoys have glass eyes.

Sometimes the body of a decoy is hollowed out. This makes the decoy lighter and easier to carry.

A piece of lead or iron is usually attached to the bottom of a decoy. This helps keep the bird upright and low in the water. Most decoys also have a ring or leather loop. An anchor line is tied to this loop.

Shore-bird decoys are carved the same way as duck decoys. Because they stand upright instead of float, shore-bird decoys don't have weights and line loops. Instead, the carver makes a hole in the base of the decoy. A stick, or leg, is inserted in this hole.

Not all decoys are solid wood. Many have cork bodies. Cork is lighter than wood, making the decoys easier to carry.

**Goose Decoys**—Some decoys, especially goose decoys, have bodies made from curved wood slats or from canvas stretched over a wood frame. Others are made from leather stuffed with cotton, straw or sand.

**Tin Decoys**—Some shore-bird decoys were made from stamped tin lithographed in bright, realistic colors.

**Silhouette Decoys**—Not all decoys have round, three-dimensional bodies. Many are *silhouettes*. They were cut out of a flat board and painted on both sides. Although they must look odd from the air, such decoys have fooled their share of waterfowl.

The manufacturer of a duck decoy is a crucial factor in determining value. The attractive redhead decoy in the background was made by an unknown carver between 1930 and 1935. It is worth $100 to $200. The white-wing scoter decoy in the foreground was created by Charles E. "Shang" Wheeler, a famous Connecticut carver. It was made between 1925 and 1930 and is worth $1,500 to $2,500.

You will often find two or three silhouettes mounted on a platform to keep them upright in the water. Examples resembling geese and crows are used for dry-land shooting. These are mounted on sticks, like shore-bird decoys.

**Owl Decoys**—These decoys were hung in trees or perched on posts around a field. They usually were made of rubber or papier-mâché. Some may have been used to lure owls. Most however, were used to frighten crows and other birds that damage crops.

**Cast-Iron Decoys**—Perhaps the strangest decoys are the cast-iron *battery decoys*. Such decoys are old. These decoys couldn't float, so commercial hunters mounted them on wood rafts called *batteries*. Commercial, or market, hunting was outlawed in 1918.

## IMPORTANT DECOY MAKERS

One important factor in determining the value of a decoy is the manufacturer. One of the first things you should do when examining a decoy is to check the base for a name or initials. Such marks may be carved, branded or stamped into the decoy. The name or initials are usually those of the original owner. However, they may also be those of the manufacturer.

Knowledgeable collectors want decoys carved by specific late 19th- and early 20th-century manufacturers. These enthusiasts will pay thousands of dollars for a decoy made by one of these masters. They will pay only a few hundred for a similar decoy by an unknown manufacturer.

**Famous Carvers**—Well-known carvers include Elmer Crowell of East Harwich, Massachusetts; Harry V. Shourds of Tuckerton, New Jersey; Charles E. "Shang" Wheeler of Stratford, Connecticut; and Steve and Lemuel Ward of Crisfield, Maryland.

Charles Schoenheider of Peoria, Illinois, and Joe Lincoln of Accord, Massachusetts, are also highly regarded.

Most decoys made by these carvers were *working decoys*. They were designed to be used by hunters.

However, some carvers began making display pieces when their creations became popular among collectors. Some of these pieces are miniatures. They are more delicate and intricately designed than working decoys. They were not intended for use in the field. Such examples can bring high prices. Display pieces by Crowell and the Ward brothers are especially valuable.

**Factory-Made Decoys**—These decoys also interest collectors. Some factory-made examples bring high prices. Well-known manufacturers include the Mason Decoy Factory and the H. A. Stevens Factory, both in Detroit, and the Wildfowler Decoy Co. of Saybrook, Connecticut. Mason decoys are especially popular with collectors. The company made three grades of decoys. The more expensive grades had more intricate carving and a more finely detailed paint job.

Condition also affects a decoy's value. Working decoys have been exposed to wind, water and sun. Some have been hit by stray lead shot. Many have pieces missing, which diminishes their value. On the other hand, decoys whose paint is somewhat worn can bring higher prices. Most decoys were repainted each year, so few have their original paint. Only a beginner would buy a freshly painted decoy or an example that has had all its paint removed.

Beyond these basic guidelines, no rules apply. If you like the way a decoy looks and can afford it, buy it! Don't let someone tell you it isn't "sculptural enough" or "lifelike enough." Most decoys are an approximate representation of a duck or shore bird. They were not made to be exact likenesses.

## COLLECTING DECOYS

Because duck and shore-bird decoys are so popular, many general antiques dealers carry them. Some specialized dealers also exist. A few very popular auctions are devoted entirely to decoys.

Decoy prices vary widely. Average-looking examples in good condition cost $50 to $100. Marked or other identifiable examples by major carvers may cost as much as $20,000. As with other collectibles, you should decide what you like and buy the best you can afford.

Beware of fakes! Early decoys have been widely reproduced during the past decade. Copies of shore-bird decoys are especially numerous. Not all reproductions are represented as authentic old decoys, but many are. Look for signs of age such as wear, cracked paint and rust on metal parts. Always get a guarantee from the seller.

Remember that decoys are still being made. Some fine examples have been produced during the past few years. Wise collectors are buying these recent creations. They are the masterworks of the future.

---

**BUYING AND SELLING
DUCK AND SHORE-BIRD DECOYS**

- A manufacturer's mark can increase the price of any decoy. Remember that many marks are those of owners or sellers, not makers. The name of an owner or seller seldom increases a decoy's value.
- Beware of fakes. If a name looks newly applied, it may be a ruse to trick you into paying a very high price for an average item.
- Know current market prices. You can keep up-to-date by reading auction results in antiques dealers' trade publications.
- Never sell a decoy by a well-known maker without checking the prevailing price.
- Where you sell a decoy helps determine its price. Decoys usually bring higher prices if they are sold in the area where they were made. You will get the best price for a decoy by a Midwestern manufacturer in the Midwest.

# FISH DECOYS, JIGS AND SPEARS

Fish decoys were used in northern states whose lakes and ponds froze in winter. Fishermen worked from shacks built on the ice. Some cut holes in the ice and lowered baited hooks into the water. These sportsmen hoped to catch such species as northern pike, pickerel and sturgeon.

Other fishermen used a different method. They impaled their prey with pitchfork-like spears. To draw the fish within range, these sportsmen used fish decoys.

These decoys resemble different species of fish. They range in length from 2 inches to 4 feet. Most are hand-carved and have tin or leather fins. They have eyes made of nailheads or glass. A large piece of lead or iron is attached to the bottom of the decoy to make it sink.

Unlike casting lures, which are discussed in the section on fishing collectibles, fish decoys have no hooks. The fisherman didn't expect the fish to snap at the decoy. He used the decoy only to entice fish within range of his spear.

A fisherman operated the decoy by lowering it through the ice on a piece of cord. The cord was attached to a short stick. A long, metal fin with several holes was attached to the back. The holes allowed the fisherman to adjust the angle at which the decoy hung in the water.

After letting the decoy sink several feet, the fisherman moved it up and down and in a circle, imitating the movements of a real fish. These movements and the color and shape of the decoy attracted fish.

When the fish were close enough, the fisherman stabbed at them with his spear. The spear was fastened to the fisherman's wrist or to the wall of the shack, so he didn't have to worry about losing his weapon in the water.

**Homemade Decoys**—Fish decoys are more varied than the fish they were intended to fool. Some are almost exact replicas of small sunfish, perch or smallmouth bass. Most, however, are like no fish that ever swam. They have red heads and white bodies, or orange polka dots on green bodies. Most people let their imaginations run wild. They make whatever they want.

**Factory-Made Decoys**—Not all fish decoys are homemade. From the 1920s to the 1940s, several small firms produced fish decoys. Some of these decoys were wood. Most were plastic or *composition,* a material comprising paper, wood pulp and glue that was used in dolls of the same period. Well-known manufacturers include Randall and Ice King. Their names are stamped on the decoys.

One commercially produced decoy even had a battery-powered light bulb inside it. The light supposedly made the decoy easier for the fish to spot!

Factory-made decoys are about six to eight inches

Sportsmen used this cast-lead jig to lure and hook large seagoing fish, such as cod and pollack. Metal jigs cost $90 to $150. They don't interest collectors as much as fish decoys, even though they are rare. This example was made about 1900.

long. Some homemade examples are much larger. Sturgeon decoys, used primarily in Wisconsin, are 24 inches to 48 inches long. These served not only as lures, but as measures. The state size limit varied from 24 inches to 40 inches. By comparing the decoy with the fish he wanted to catch, a sportsman could determine whether the fish was within the legal size limits.

**Fish Jigs** — Don't confuse fish decoys with fish jigs. Some jigs are shaped like fish. Others are triangular or rectangular. Jigs are made of lead or copper. They have one or more hooks attached to the head or nose. Jigs are usually used in saltwater fishing. After being lowered deep in the water, they are jerked, or *jigged,* up and down. Such fish as cod, halibut and pollack mistake the fluttering jig for a small, tasty fish.

Most collectors are interested only in jigs that look like real fish. Triangular or rectangular jigs may serve the same purpose, but they lack the folksy charm of the fish-shaped examples. There are fewer types of fish jigs than fish decoys. Most collectors prefer the decoys.

## COLLECTING FISH DECOYS, JIGS AND SPEARS

Fish decoys and jigs were made and used in a limited area. Decoys were produced primarily in Minnesota, Michigan, Wisconsin, New York and northern New England. Jigs were used by New England fishermen, especially those who fished the Grand Banks area.

The supply of fish decoys is slowly dwindling. Most states have outlawed ice fishing with a spear. Therefore, few fish decoys are being made. Most collectible examples were manufactured between 1900 and 1950.

Even so, fish decoys are not hard to find. Within the past decade, they have become popular with collectors and antique dealers. They are available in many areas of the country.

However, if you want to acquire fish decoys, you should take a trip to the Great Lakes region. You can find excellent examples at auctions and antique shops. You might also find a wonderful bargain in a fisherman's barn.

Because many types of fish decoys are available, you may decide to specialize. You could collect only factory-made decoys. The most valuable examples are those that still have their original boxes, advertising literature and other go-withs.

You could collect only fish decoys resembling one type of fish, such as sturgeon or sunfish. You could acquire decoys made or used in one state or made by one craftsman. Collecting by craftsman is challenging because few carvers signed their work.

You could collect unusual decoys, such as frogs or turtles. These are very interesting and rare.

Fish or eel spears are excellent additions to a fish-decoy collection. Most date from 1850 to 1920 and are made of hand-wrought iron. They have three to six

tines. A few have iron handles, but most have a socket into which a wood pole was fixed. They rarely carry a manufacturer's name.

Fish spears have an interesting shape. Some collectors mount them on a wood or iron base, as they would a sculpture.

Fish jigs are harder to find than decoys or spears. Most fishermen believed that if a jig had the right motion, it didn't need to look like a fish. As a result, jigs shaped like fish are somewhat rare. The best sources are dealers along the New England coast.

Remember that many enthusiasts regard these objects as folk art. You are more likely to find these items in art galleries than in shops specializing in antique fishing tackle.

Prices for most mementos are reasonable. You can buy small fish decoys for $20 to $50. Larger examples, from 18 inches to 48 inches, cost $100 to $800. Fish spears usually cost $15 to $50. Jigs cost as much as $150, depending on their shape. Most jigs cost much less because few collectors are interested in them.

<br>

---

### BUYING AND SELLING FISH DECOYS, JIGS AND SPEARS

- Bigger is better. Large decoys are more valuable than small ones. Manufacturers made fewer large decoys because such decoys were used primarily to attract sturgeon, which are scarce. If you have to choose between buying an 18-inch-long decoy or several smaller specimens, buy the large item. You won't be sorry.
- Select well-carved examples. Accurate coloration is not as important. Many fish decoys were painted in fanciful colors.
- Look for rare forms, such as frogs, turtles and giant grasshoppers.
- Don't be fooled by people who remove the hooks from oversized fishing lures. Lures are less valuable than decoys. You can easily tell them apart. Lures have holes or patches where the hooks were removed.

---

These wrought-iron spears are mounted like pieces of sculpture. They date from 1860 to 1930 and cost $35 to $100 each. These spears were used on eels and fish.

19th century bicycles are rare and expensive. This so-called *bone crusher,* an adult tricycle 5 feet high at the handlebars, is worth more than $5,000. It was made about 1870. Later examples cost $50 to $500.

# BICYCLING, ICE-SKATING, ROLLER-SKATING AND SKIING COLLECTIBLES

Bicycling, ice skating, roller skating and skiing are entertaining ways to travel. This is only part of their appeal. These activities are also highly competitive sports. Bicycle races are an important part of the Summer Olympics. Skiing and ice skating form the heart of the Winter Olympics. The roller derby is very popular in several parts of the country.

Numerous mementos are associated with these sports. Many collectors are former participants. Interest in the activity leads to interest in collecting its memorabilia.

## BICYCLING

The first bicycles appeared during the early 1800s. They were called *velocipedes,* Latin for *speedy foot.* Most were uncomfortable and impractical. One version had iron tires with wood rims!

The invention of lighter, safer bicycles in the 1880s revolutionized the sport. During the next 15 years, bicycling became extremely popular in the United States. Cycling clubs, whose members were called *wheelmen,* were established throughout the country. Day tours of up to 100 miles were common for men and women. Match races for sizable purses were also popular.

All this seemed to vanish when the automobile appeared. It was not until the early 1970s that bicycles regained their popularity. The sensational Olympic racing triumphs of 1984 are proof that American cycling has returned to its former glory.

## COLLECTING BICYCLES

Collecting antique bicycles is serious business. Many bicycle enthusiasts are knowledgeable and wealthy.

Early *bone crushers,* high-wheeled bikes with solid rubber tires and no springs, cost as much as $5,000 at auction. Valuable 19th-century bicycles include the *ordinary*, known in England as the *penny farthing*. This has a large front wheel and a tiny back wheel. Mark Twain owned an ordinary. You can see it at his former home in Hartford, Connecticut.

Bicycles built for two and adult tricycles are also popular.

Some 20th-century bicycles are highly prized. Those made by obscure or short-lived manufacturers are especially valuable. Bicycles with unusual design elements also bring high prices. Collectors want working examples in excellent condition.

If you plan to restore an old bicycle, use authentic parts. Additions or alterations greatly reduce a bicycle's value.

## MISCELLANEOUS BICYCLING COLLECTIBLES

Many interesting items are associated with bicycling. Some people collect equipment, such as the once-mandatory trouser clips. Some clips are sterling silver. Tire pumps, rearview mirrors, reflectors, lights, and early carrying baskets and saddlebags are also collectible.

Many enthusiasts buy bicycling ephemera. This includes rare programs, posters, books and magazines.

Cycling clubs of the 1880s and 1890s produced numerous collectibles. These include itineraries issued by wheelmen for their day-long trips. Clubs also issued shoulder patches, handlebar tags, caps, jackets and banners.

Trophies are also collectible. They are usually sterling silver, silver plate or bronze. Many are very attractive. Some have pictures of riders in appropriate costumes on vintage bicycles.

## ICE SKATING

The Dutch began skating in the 16th century. One hundred years later, the Dutchmen of New Amsterdam, now called New York City, were continuing the custom. Early skates were made of shaped bone. By the 1600s, wood skates with curving iron runners were being used. The modern steel-runner skate did not appear until the late 1800s.

## COLLECTING ICE SKATES

Collectors are most interested in ice skates made from 1860 to 1910. These skates had to be bound to the shoe with leather thongs. The runners were made of thin wrought-iron. The runners sometimes were capped by a tiny brass ball.

These interesting, attractive artifacts cost less than $50 a pair. They look lovely displayed on a wall.

Shoe skates with steel runners appeared in the early 20th century. Enthusiasts have not been interested in most of these skates. The exceptions have been skates worn by famous hockey players or figure skaters.

## ICE-SKATING EPHEMERA

Most books and magazines about ice skating were published in this century. They are inexpensive and easy to locate.

Programs for ice-skating races and figure-skating competitions are not popular with collectors. Neither are race tickets or advertising posters. Such items are often hard to find, but they offer excellent opportunities for beginning collectors.

## ROLLER SKATING

Roller skating requires large, hard, smooth surfaces. Therefore, it was not until the late 19th century that the idea of putting wheels on shoes became a reality. When smoothly paved streets and buildings with large wood floors appeared, skaters came out in droves.

## COLLECTING ROLLER SKATES

The oldest available roller skates are the clamp-on type made at the turn of the century. Shoe skates were not popular until the 1920s. Modern roller skates with adjustment screws and braking devices were not made until 30 years ago.

The keys used to adjust clamp-on roller skates are interesting collectibles. Some keys are silver or bronze. Because they are small and easily displayed, skate keys are becoming more popular.

## ROLLER-SKATING EPHEMERA

Few books about roller skating exist. However, some periodicals cover the sport. Several magazines are devoted exclusively to roller derby. This spectator sport, famous for its theatrical violence, was most popular during the 1950s and 1960s. Roller-derby posters, advertising materials and ticket stubs comprise an interesting and untapped field for adventurous collectors. Roller-derby enthusiasts look for uniforms, shoulder patches, jerseys and other clothing worn by players.

## SKIING

Skis were used centuries ago in Scandinavia for transportation. Skis more than 4,000 years old have been discovered there. Some were made of smoothed-down animal bones. The sport of skiing was founded in Norway in the 19th century. In 1872, the first ski club was formed in the United States. Since then, skiing has enjoyed great popularity. The Winter Olympics has increased interest in the sport.

## COLLECTING SKIS

Early collectible skis are made of wood, usually a hardwood such as ash, maple or birch. The earliest examples have simple leather straps to hold the skis on a person's feet.

Vintage roller skates cost $5 to $10 per pair. These skates date from 1930 to 1940. Most examples are marked with the name of a manufacturer, such as the Union Hardware Co., Torrington, Conn.

Very few 19th-century American skis are available. Most skis found in collections were made between 1900 and 1940. These items resemble modern cross-country skis. However, they are heavier and much wider. This is because they were used in the period before chairlifts. Skiers had to climb up hills before skiing down.

Collectors will soon begin acquiring contemporary steel and plastic skis. The design of these skis has changed rapidly during the past decade. Some examples, especially those made in limited quantities, are already hard to find.

Modern ski bindings were not available until after World War II. Early examples are collectible.

## MISCELLANEOUS SKIING COLLECTIBLES

Look for programs, ticket stubs, posters and similar paper goods. Equipment, such as goggles, caps, jackets and early ski boots are also collectible.

Ski patches issued by various resorts are especially appealing. These items are avidly sought by young collectors. Also look for metal and ceramic badges sold at ski slopes.

Enthusiasts are eagerly compiling runs of contemporary skiing magazines. These will be very valuable in a few years.

Autographs of world-class skiers are highly prized. Trophies awarded to the winners of ski meets are also valuable.

## COLLECTING BICYCLING, ICE-SKATING, ROLLER-SKATING, AND SKIING MEMORABILIA

If you are interested in one of these areas, your opportunities are almost unlimited. Because these hobbies are relatively new, you will have to work harder to develop expertise. But that can make the search more exciting.

Old bicycles, ice skates, roller skates and skis can be found in out-of-the-way places. Look in attics, sheds and old sporting-goods stores. Garage sales sometimes yield treasures. Advertising in collectors' publications and local newspapers can bring surprising results.

Old bicycles and ice skates are carried by some antique dealers. However, skiing and roller-skating memorabilia are hard to find. You will seldom find them at shows, shops or auctions. If you are interested in skiing and ice-skating mementos, take a trip through the northern states. Such items were used every day in this area during winter.

Roller skating and bicycling mementos can be found throughout the country. Most were used by children, and the things children outgrow become tomorrow's collectibles. Prices for most items are reasonable. Choose carefully. Don't pay a high price for a damaged bicycle or a pair of rusty skates. Better examples will come along.

At $1 to $2 each, vintage skate keys are an excellent bargain. They are easy to display and are guaranteed to bring back memories of bruised knees and bumpy sidewalks. These examples were made between 1930 and 1940.

Enameled metal ski pins are popular new collectibles. They are sold at all major American and European resorts. Most date from 1970 to the present and cost $3 to $5 each. Several hundred have been made, and new ones are issued each year.

# OTHER SPORTS COLLECTIBLES

The field of sports memorabilia is limited only by the number of sports. Some lesser-known sports offer great opportunities for collectors.

## ARCHERY

At one time, the longbow and arrow were important weapons and hunting tools. After firearms were created, the longbow and its mechanical counterpart, the crossbow, became sporting devices.

Archery was revived as a competitive sport in the 1860s. Within 20 years, it was extremely popular in the United States. Clubs of bowmen and bowwomen sponsored competitions.

The crossbow was seldom used in this country, but the longbow is still used for sport and hunting. Collectibles in the field include early bows, arrows, wrist guards, quivers and trophies.

## BADMINTON

Badminton was a popular sport for women during the 19th century. It developed from an East Indian game called *poona.* Badminton was brought to the United States from England during the 1890s. It was an immediate hit as a lawn game.

Few old badminton sets have survived. Collectors must be content with rackets and birds, called *shuttlecocks,* made from 1920 to 1940. Early shuttlecocks had real feathers and cork-and-rubber bases. They are valuable collectibles. Early nets and poles are hard to find. The best way to locate these items is to advertise in local newspapers and collectors' publications.

## BILLIARDS

During the 19th century, billiards was the preeminent indoor game for men. Every town had its pool hall, and a well-to-do gentleman had a billiards room in his home.

Despite its popularity, billiards offers few

Pool and billiards memorabilia include a two-piece billiards cue in maple and ivory, $65 to $80; a set of early ceramic billiards balls in a wood triangle, $75 to $100; a set of toy ceramic billiards balls in a tin triangle, $35 to $50; and a copy of *The Judge* magazine from 1883, featuring a cartoon of billiards players, $55 to $75.

mementos. Most collectors buy *cues,* the tapered, leather-tipped sticks used to strike the balls. Some old cues are spectacular. They are made of ebony or other precious hardwood, and are inlaid with silver. Some have tortoise-shell or ivory handles.

Early billiards balls are also collectible. Today's examples are made of composition, but old balls were made of elephant ivory!

Other billiards collectibles include tables, ball frames and ball racks. Tables can be very elaborate and expensive. Examples in good condition cost several thousand dollars.

## BOATING AND SAILING

Many Americans own boats, and motorboating and sailing are popular fair-weather pastimes. Numerous collectibles are associated with these activities.

Yachting enthusiasts have a great deal from which to choose. Currier & Ives prints of the famous America's Cup races are very popular. Small cigarette cards featuring famous Victorian actresses wearing the colors of various boat clubs are also collectible. Some collectors acquire trophies. Others buy articles used aboard yachts.

Powerboat aficionados collect pictures, programs and souvenirs associated with speedboat races of the 1930s and 1940s.

Other collectibles include boat flags and pennants. These are attractive and easy to display. Compasses, tillers, wheels and other types of equipment are also popular.

Don't overlook the many boat models made during the 19th and 20th centuries. Some of these are five feet long, and may cost thousands of dollars.

Books and magazines about sailing and boat racing are also collectible.

## BOWLING

A form of bowling called *nine pins* was popular in 17th-century New York City, known in those days as New Amsterdam. The Dutch played it in the streets! As you may remember from the section on golf, those streets were also full of golfers. New Amsterdam must have been a lively town.

Modern bowling with tenpins and specific rules was invented in the 1890s. Today, bowling is perhaps the most popular indoor participation sport in the United States.

Sailing collectibles include sterling-silver cigarette box given as a regatta prize in 1961, $45 to $60; a nickel-plated cast-iron anchor paperweight from the 1950s, $25 to $30; and a reproduction Currier & Ives sailing lithograph, $35 to $40. Because Currier & Ives originals are so expensive, many collectors buy 20th-century reprints.

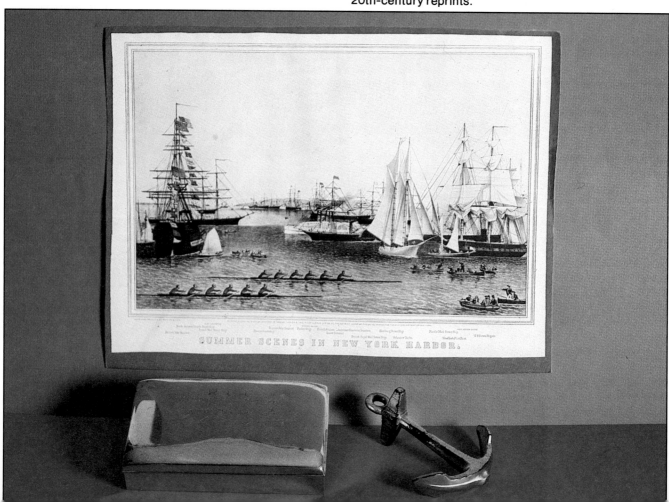

SUMMER SCENES IN NEW YORK HARBOR.

The most popular collectibles are bowling balls. Look for old wood ones. Pins are also interesting. They come in various shapes and colors. You can also assemble collections of score cards from famous matches. Enthusiasts buy bowling shirts, shoes and trophies. Ephemera includes posters, pictures and magazines.

## BOXING

The "manly art of self-defense" has played a prominent role in the American sporting scene for a long time. Boxing was popular in this country before 1800. However, it was not until the second half of the 19th century that gloves were introduced and rules established.

Some people consider the sport cruel, but boxing has many fans and collectibles. The most popular mementos are championship belts, gloves and trunks worn by great fighters. These are hard to find and expensive. A robe worn by Joe Louis costs thousands of dollars.

Most enthusiasts collect ephemera. Many posters, programs, autographs, score cards and pictures remain as souvenirs of the great fights and fighters of the past century.

Don't forget the collectors' cards produced by Topps and other companies. They are less popular than baseball and football cards, and can usually be purchased for a few cents apiece.

## BULLFIGHTING

Like boxing, bullfighting has its fans and foes. Although never practiced in this country, many Americans have been fascinated by *la fiesta brava.* Its greatest fans have included such literary giants as Ernest Hemingway.

Enthusiasts collect swords; the *traje de luces,* or *suit of lights,* worn by matadors; large capes, or *capotes;* and *muletas,* small bits of cloth the matadors use to make daring passes at the bull.

Ephemera is one of the most popular types of bullfighting memento. Books, posters, programs and ticket stubs are all collectible.

## CROQUET

Very few sports were open to both men and women during the 19th century. The gentle game of croquet, introduced in the United States in the 1860s, was one of these. Because it offered opportunities for young men and women to get together, it was called *the courting game.*

Croquet is a lawn game that requires little equipment. It was an instant success and is popular today. Collectors look for the mallets, balls, stakes and wickets used in the game. Some of these are very attractive. The miniature, or table, games are also popular. These were designed to be used in winter, when lawns were not available.

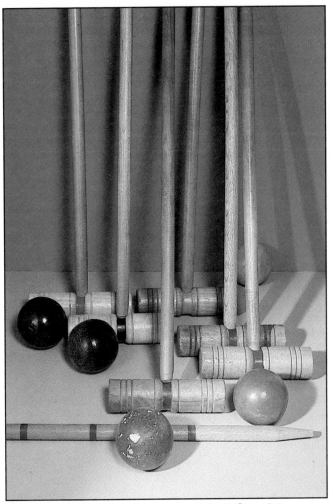

Croquet mallets and balls are easy to find. Complete sets and miniature table-top sets should increase in value. The items shown here cost $10 to $15 per set and date from 1920 to 1940.

## FENCING

Swordsmanship was once considered a necessary skill for many men. After modern weapons replaced the sword, it became a sporting device. Fencing matches were part of the first modern Olympic games. Today, fencing has many fans throughout the world.

The masks and body padding used in fencing interest some collectors. However, most enthusiasts look for dueling swords. These include the rapier, foil, epee and saber.

Because fencing is less popular in the United States than in Europe, American collectors can find bargains. Late 19th- or 20th-century equipment bought in the United States costs a fraction of what it might in Europe.

Remember that fencing swords, like firearms, are potentially dangerous. Use discretion in storing and displaying these items.

## HORSE RACING AND RIDING

Horse racing has been a popular American sport for centuries. The first course was laid out on Long Island, New York, during the 1660s.

At first, racing involved men riding saddled horses around a flat track. By the late 19th century, trotting and pacing events featuring horse-drawn carriages, or *sulkies,* had become popular.

Mementos of flat-track and sulky racing abound. You can find everything from *racing silks,* the caps and blouses worn by jockeys or drivers, to saddles. Even sulkies are available.

Another type of riding has its own history and memorabilia. This is show riding, exemplified by the National Horse Show. This important event has been held annually in New York City since 1885. Show-riding mementos include saddles, stirrups, crops, bits and bridles, and other equipment. Posters and programs for major events are also popular.

Don't forget rodeo. This sport, reminiscent of the American West, has its own heroes and memorabilia. You can acquire saddles, ropes, spurs and elaborate trophies. Belt buckles are especially popular.

Fox hunting is another type of riding. Although few people participate in this sport, many collectors are familiar with it. The colorful jackets and hats worn by hunters make interesting collectibles. The horns used to signal the hunt are also attractive. The silver stirrup cups that the hunters used to toast themselves and the hunt are charming mementos.

## POLO

Polo was introduced in the United States during the 1870s. Few Americans are familiar with the game. The field on which the game is played is so large that it makes polo unsuitable as a spectator sport. Polo horses are so expensive that only the wealthy can afford to participate.

Polo collectibles include the long-handled mallets and balls with which the game is played. Some enthusiasts also acquire team jerseys.

## SOCCER

Long popular in Europe and Latin America, soccer has attracted national attention in the United States during the past decade. The introduction of professional leagues has resulted in the production of collectibles such as uniforms, programs and ticket stubs. Balls signed by well-known players such as Pélé are valuable but hard to find.

## COLLECTING OTHER SPORTS MEMORABILIA

Some sports, such as boxing and horse racing, are popular with collectors. To find mementos, you will have to attend auctions and visit specialized shops. You may have to pay substantial sums for what you want. But don't let the popularity of these sports discourage you. Many opportunities exist for the canny collector.

Most of these sports have not yet attracted great collector interest. Therefore, you are more likely to find the items at garage sales and secondhand stores than at antique shows or memorabilia shops. Until there is more demand for mementos associated with these sports, you will have to use your ingenuity to find items you want. This can be the most exciting way to build a collection.

---

### BUYING AND SELLING OTHER SPORTS COLLECTIBLES

- Because few of these items have attracted collectors' attention, prices are low. However, many items are difficult to find. Publications related to the field are good sources.
- Other collectors can help you. They may compete with you for some items, but you will often be interested in different things. Each person can look for items that interest other collectors. Then you can buy or swap. Swapping is one of the best ways to add to your collection. If done fairly, both collectors benefit.

---

Among the most prized mementos of the bullring is the heavy cape, or *capote,* used by the matador in the first stages of the fight. This example was made during the 1950s and is worth $75 to $100. Had it been used by an important matador, it would be worth much more.

Bullfighting ephemera is popular. Clockwise from upper left: hand cards passed out in the street, 1968, $10 to $15 each; posters, 1964, $20 to $200, depending on size and condition; programs, 1968, $25 to $50 each; ticket stubs, 1963, $2 to $3 each.

# Building a Collection

One exciting aspect of collecting sports memorabilia is the number of categories to choose from. Some categories, such as sporting firearms and duck decoys, are extremely popular. Collectors compete for many items and prices are high. Other categories have been virtually untouched. These include golf, tennis and bowling memorabilia. If you choose one of these areas, you will be a pioneer. Your explorations will yield many rewards, including numerous interesting mementos at very low prices.

You may feel intimidated by the number and types of items you can buy. What should you collect? The answer is, you should buy mementos you like, can afford and can display in an appealing manner.

Your interests and your home will help determine what you collect. If you have been a bowler or tennis player, old bowling balls or tennis rackets may be interesting to acquire. If you live in a small apartment, you probably won't collect vintage bicycles, no matter how much you like cycling.

The following information is designed to help you make decisions about collecting.

## CHOOSING A CATEGORY

The type of sports memorabilia you decide to collect will probably reflect your personal experience. Many people started collecting memorabilia related to a sport they participated in. Other collectors have never been participants. Thanks to television, thousands of fans enjoy their favorite sports in their own homes. Many of these enthusiasts decorate their homes with mementos associated with the sports they watch.

### COLLECT WHAT YOU LIKE

You may already have some items related to your favorite sport or sports. *Favorite* is the key word here. You should collect what you favor—what you like. There are other factors to consider, but the most important concern in building a collection should be personal satisfaction. If it doesn't give you pleasure, no amount of financial value or prestige can really justify its existence.

### COLLECT WHAT YOU CAN AFFORD

Other than personal satisfaction, perhaps the most important factor in selecting a category is cost.

How much can you afford to invest in your collection? Are enough inexpensive items available? Can you assemble a satisfying collection without hurting yourself financially?

Before you choose a category, make sure you can afford it. Some categories have numerous inexpensive items. Some have both reasonably priced and costly items. A few have mostly *high-ticket* items, which are very expensive.

Baseball cards comprise a good category for beginning collectors and those of modest means. Thousands of cards made during the 1970s and 1980s are available, and most are very reasonably priced. Many baseball cards can be purchased for 50 cents each. They cost even less when you buy them in quantity.

Some cards are rare and expensive, but you can build a large and interesting collection without them. You may never have to pay more than a few dollars for a card.

Most categories of sports memorabilia have both inexpensive and costly items. Fishing memorabilia is a good example. You can find hundreds of lures, plugs, spoons and flies made between 1920 and 1950 that cost less than $5 each. However, if you want early bamboo fly rods, you will have to pay much more. Examples by such legendary manufacturers as Hiram Leonard or Edward Payne sometimes cost $1,000 or more each.

The category of antique hunting rifles has mostly high-ticket items. The least expensive hunting rifle costs several hundred dollars. Examples made during the 19th-century cost thousands.

### DISPLAY AND STORAGE

Another consideration when selecting a category is the size of your home. How much space do you have for displaying and storing your collection?

Think carefully about this before you start collecting. Are items in your chosen category too big for the space available? Perhaps you can compromise. You

Press pins and sports jewelry include a U.S. Golf Association press pin; Basketball Writers Association membership pin; press pin for the 1962 World Series featuring the New York Yankees; membership pin for the Football Writers Association of America; Professional Golfers Association press pin; CBS Sports U.S. Open pin; National Hockey League press pin; pair of baseball cuff links; U.S. Golf Association stickpin. The press pins are worth $25 to $75 each. The jewelry, which is gold-filled, costs $50 to $85.

may decide to collect pictures of famous racehorses instead of saddles or bridles. Even if you have to change your collection slightly, you'll still have fun. Remember that showing your mementos to family and friends is one of the most enjoyable aspects of collecting. You won't have as much fun if you can't display your acquisitions.

## LIMITING YOUR COLLECTION

The amount of display and storage space you have will limit the number of objects in your collection. However, regardless of the space available, you should limit your collection anyway. If you select too large a field, your hobby will become overwhelming, and you will become discouraged.

Don't try to collect an example of every type of sports memorabilia in every category. It's impossible. Collecting every item in one category could take a lifetime.

You can use several techniques to limit your collection. One is to buy one type of item. Rather than collecting all types of fishing memorabilia, collect only wood casting plugs. Hundreds of different plugs are available. In a few years, you could assemble an impressive collection.

Be careful not to narrow your collection too much. If you decide to collect only 19th-century autographed baseballs, you will have a very small collection. You might have to wait months or years for each new addition.

## COLLECT THE BEST

Perhaps the most important guideline is this: Buy the best things you can afford. *Best* can mean many things. It can refer to the oldest or rarest items, or those that are most attractive or in mint condition. Try to buy items that meet these standards.

Knowledgeable collectors and dealers agree that $10 spent on a single good item is a wiser investment than $10 spent on several less-desirable items. The more expensive piece will appreciate in value more rapidly than the less desirable pieces. Furthermore, you may not find the expensive memento again. Ordinary and damaged examples are always available.

## COLLECTING BY CATEGORY

Most collectibles can be categorized by sport. However, subcategories of memorabilia exist within each sport.

For example, you may decide to collect fishing rods, reels, lures and accessories.

Such a collection could rapidly become very large. You then might decide to narrow your focus. You might collect only reels or rods. However, each of these subcategories contains hundreds of variations. To limit your collection even further, you could concentrate on rods or reels made by a single manufacturer.

Membership pins for hunting and fishing clubs cost $2 to $5 each. Such pins are inexpensive and easy to find. Most collectors specialize in pins from one state. The examples shown here were made between 1930 and 1980.

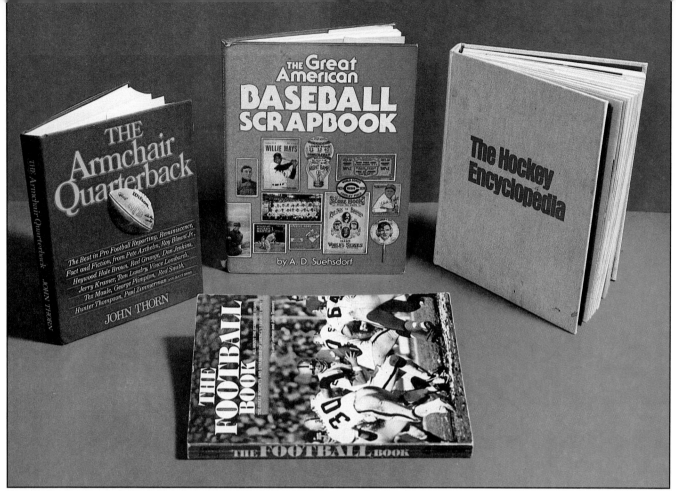

Sports books are an interesting specialty. These books on baseball, football and hockey date from the 1970s and sell for $10 to $15 each.

Sports ephemera includes a New York Yankees program, early 1980s, $2 to $4; booklet on tennis star Bjorn Borg, 1970s, $6 to $8; 1978 U.S. Open program, $5 to $7; 1972 edition of *Prolog,* the National Football League's annual publication, $10 to $13.

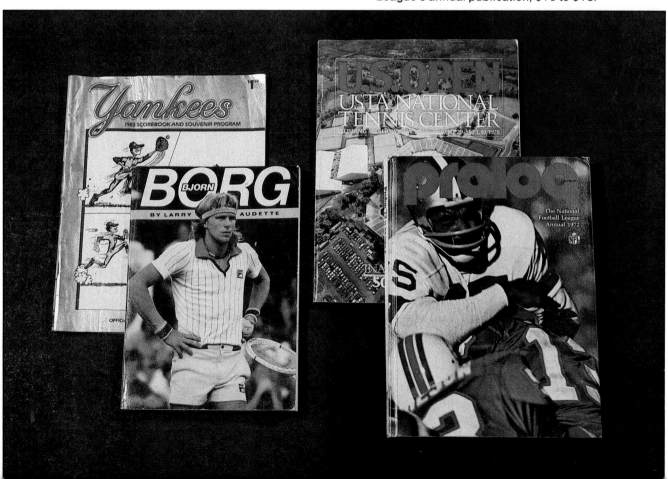

Or you might choose another alternative. You could collect examples of each type of fishing gear produced by one famous manufacturer. You could buy products made by South Bend or Orvis. Such a collection would include rods, reels, lures, bait boxes, nets and creels.

This strategy is especially popular with duck-decoy collectors. Many decoys were made by individuals. The products of famous carvers such as Ira Hudson and Joseph Lincoln cost thousands of dollars each. Decoys made by unknown manufacturers may cost less than $50 apiece.

Collecting sports memorabilia by manufacturer is relatively easy. It is more difficult to do this with other collectibles, such as furniture and bottles. The reason is simple. Most sports mementos were produced by firms that marked their products. These firms also marked the containers in which their products were sold. Manufacturers of other collectibles frequently did not do this.

If you collect the products of one sporting-goods manufacturer, your collection may be very expensive. You may discover that the manufacturer made everything from tennis rackets to trout flies to bowling balls.

Categories should not become straitjackets. They are meant to free you, not restrain you. Categories are designed to help you think about how to approach collecting. As you add to your collection, you will want to change it. You will add new pieces and drop others. You will broaden or narrow the limits of your acquisitions as you become more experienced.

## COLLECTING BY PERIOD

As your collection grows, you will probably find yourself more interested in older items. If you choose to collect fishing reels, you will probably begin by purchasing ordinary, readily available examples. Most will date from the 1930s and 1940s. In time, you will probably start looking for late 19th- and early 20th-century examples. These are more difficult to find and are more expensive.

In most cases, collecting older items means collecting fewer. A limited number of older examples have survived. They are usually costly and rare. They are sought by the most seasoned and wily collectors.

This scenario won't occur with new, less-popular categories. There is little competition for tennis and golf

Steel wool and cleansing powder will do wonders for rusted metal sports collectibles such as this old golf club. Use a commercial rust remover if necessary.

Garages, attics and cellars are good places to look for sports collectibles. Mementos are often stored in such places and then forgotten for decades.

memorabilia. You can acquire 19th-century examples in good condition very inexpensively.

No hard-and-fast rules exist regarding age categories for sports memorabilia. However, most collectors recognize three general periods. These are pre-1900, pre-World War II and post-World War II.

Most pre-1900 objects date from the 1880s and 1890s. Earlier examples are rare. Objects made between 1900 and the end of World War II are in greatest demand. They are fairly easy to find and are old enough to have an appealing "antique" look. Post-World War II mementos are easy to find but are less interesting to some collectors. These enthusiasts believe items made after World War II are not old enough. However, some items, such as Super Bowl tickets, were not made before World War II.

If you are collecting items by period, don't become obsessed with age for its own sake. Some of the most interesting sports mementos were produced during the last few decades. It would be a mistake to ignore these pieces just because they are not old.

## MAKING YOUR COLLECTION UNIQUE

Every enthusiast has the opportunity to establish a unique collection. You will learn about new categories as you talk to other aficionados, attend shows and read specialized material. You will probably develop your own approach to collecting. However, you should remember a few guidelines:

**Choose Categories Carefully**—Collecting categories should be neither too broad nor too narrow. If your category is too extensive, you may quickly run out of space and money. You may never have the chance to assemble a representative collection. If your category is too narrow, you may go months or years without being able to add anything new.

The ideal collecting category allows for reasonable and orderly expansion. Your collection should give you pleasure at every stage, whether you own one item or 200.

**Calculate Cost**—Keep prices in mind. Some categories of sports memorabilia are very expensive. You may love 19th-century sporting rifles or duck decoys by master carvers, but. you may not be able to afford them. Such items often cost thousands of dollars. Many interesting, less expensive items are available.

**Think of Investment Potential**—Be aware of the value of your collectibles. You are probably collecting sports memorabilia as a hobby, not as an investment. Even so, your collection may become very valuable. Antiques and collectibles often increase in value more rapidly than stocks or bonds. They have done so recently, and it is reasonable to assume that this trend will continue.

**Buy the Best**—Always buy the finest pieces you can afford, especially if you are interested in the investment potential of your acquisitions. Rarity, age and condition are always important factors. Go with quality, but be sure to buy mementos that you like. Collecting should be fun as well as profitable.

**Upgrade Your Collection**—As you acquire more pieces and learn more about your chosen area, you may want to change the focus of your collection. The first things you bought may no longer appeal to you. They may seem too ordinary, too badly damaged or too ugly. Get rid of them! Sell them, trade them or donate them to local charity auctions. Such donations are tax deductible.

Experienced collectors are always improving their collections, even when it means reducing the number of mementos they have. It is always better to own 100 outstanding items than 500 run-of-the-mill examples.

## FINDING SPORTS COLLECTIBLES

Collectors have many opportunities to find mementos. Locating what you want requires knowledge and luck. The more knowledgeable you are, the luckier you will be.

**Check Storage Areas**—Many sports collectibles can be found in attics, storage sheds and basements. Be sure to check secondhand stores. You may find mementos such as golf clubs, tennis rackets, bowling balls and old bicycles in any of these places. Because few people know such items are collectible, these mementos are frequently stored away and forgotten. You may find excellent bargains.

**Check Garage Sales**—These sales frequently include desirable items. No matter what you see displayed,

A split, such as the one in the shaft of this 1920 bamboo ski pole, is a major flaw. The shaft can be glued together with epoxy. Never pay a high price for equipment in this condition.

NFL jewelry and pins can be fun to collect and wear.

always ask about the objects you want. Questions such as "Do you have any old hunting and fishing magazines?" or "Any books about sports around?" may result in an excellent buy. People holding garage sales usually put out what they don't want and what they think others will buy. They may not realize that you might want that old tin box full of fishing lures. They may not have remembered to bring down that old sailing trophy from the attic. It is your responsibility to let them know what you want.

**Advertise**—A short notice in local newspapers asking for "old baseball and football pennants or programs" or "pictures of horses" may bring surprising results. Keep your ad short and simple. You want people to know exactly what you are seeking. If you are looking for several different items, advertise for them one at a time. That way, you can change your ad every few weeks and keep it fresh.

**Talk with Dealers**—You can't expect to find everything you want at yard sales or in secondhand shops. Few people are naive enough to sell a decoy for $2 or a silver-plated yachting trophy for $5. The more widely known the collectible, the greater the competition to acquire it.

If you are seeking popular items, you will have to check with dealers, auction houses and other collectors.

Many antique dealers carry some sports mementos. Some antique dealers have sports memorabilia and don't realize it. For example, the loving cups awarded to winners of sports events often are sold to silver dealers.

Flea market and antique dealers are beginning to stock golf, tennis, fishing and other sports memorabilia. The shops or show booths of dealers specializing in paper collectibles are good places to find baseball and football cards. Such dealers may also sell sports programs, sports magazines and posters.

Don't expect to find many dealers specializing in sports memorabilia. A few dealers specialize in guns or sporting prints and paintings. However, such dealers play only a small role in the field of sports memorabilia.

The best thing to do is to let a few reputable dealers know exactly what you are looking for. Then wait for them to call you. The more dealers you become acquainted with, the more help you will receive.

**Talk with Collectors**—Some enthusiasts have special cards printed with their name, address and a statement explaining what they collect. Typical statements include

Magazines, programs, posters and other ephemera should be stored in acid-resistant sleeves such as these. Be sure to keep collectibles away from water and dampness.

"Collector of fishing reels" and "Always looking for pre-1900 horse-racing memorabilia." Collectors give these cards to people at antique shows and to owners of antique shops and secondhand stores. If you hand out enough cards, you may find this technique is an effective way to find new acquisitions.

As you become more knowledgeable, you will discover that the best sources for new acquisitions are other enthusiasts. Experienced collectors are often more knowledgeable about their areas of interest than antique dealers or even museum employees. They can provide you with important information and valuable acquisitions. Try to meet or correspond with other enthusiasts. Let them know what you are interested in.

You can meet other collectors at antique shows and auctions and through collectors' clubs. Even if they don't share your particular interest, collectors will often watch for items you want. You can do the same for them. In that way, collecting becomes a type of team sport.

**Attend Auctions**—Auctions can be wonderful sources for some types of collectibles, but they are not reliable sources for sports memorabilia.

Auctions devoted entirely to sports items are extremely rare. Auctioneers usually recognize the value of popular items such as duck decoys. However, they may not recognize the value of other sports mementos. When something other than a well-known item is found in a general estate, it may go unnoticed. It may not even be mentioned in the auctioneer's advertisement.

The best thing to do is tell several auctioneers what you are looking for. They will let you know when such pieces appear in an estate they are working with.

Be sure to attend pre-auction exhibitions, called *viewings*. You may be the only person to spot a valuable item. This is the positive side of the indifference many people feel toward sports memorabilia. When a choice item does appear at a local auction house, its value may not be recognized. You may not have much competition when you bid for it.

## BUYING AND SELLING SPORTS COLLECTIBLES

Many collectors find a few pieces in attics or barns. Some receive a few mementos as gifts. However, most enthusiasts purchase the majority of the items in their collections. An understanding of the collectible and antique markets can help you buy more wisely.

**Supply and Demand**—The prices of antiques and collectibles are determined principally by supply and demand. A rare duck decoy in good condition is expensive. Many collectors are interested in this field, and choice pieces are hard to find.

A baseball card from the 1950s may also be sought by numerous collectors, but it costs just a few dollars. Why? Because the card is one of thousands. More cards are available than collectors.

On the other hand, a rare, 1890 jockey's cap may have a low price because few collectors want it.

**Three Basic Guidelines**—To understand prices, you must know about trends in your field. You can learn about current prices in three basic ways. One is to read price guides, such as the one in this book. The second is to attend auctions and see how much sports mementos are selling for. The third way is to check dealers' prices.

Pricing is not an exact science. You will find different prices for similar items. However, if you check all three sources, you will have a good idea of the item's value.

**Getting the Best Price**—If you want to sell mementos, you will probably get less than the current market price. A dealer can seldom pay you more than 50% to 70% of the going price. This is because dealers must cover their overhead and also make a profit.

A collector can pay more than a dealer. If you sell to a collector, you can usually ask the going rate. But most collectors negotiate, so you will probably have to lower the price to consummate the sale.

If you sell an item at auction, you may get more than the market price. However, you will have to pay the auction house a commission, usually 10% to 20% of the selling price. You must pay this commission even if the memento sells for less than the market price.

Never sell a piece from your collection without knowing its approximate value. Even if you don't like the item, it may be worth a great deal of money. If price guides and dealers can't help you establish a price, call an expert. The expert's fee will be an added expense. But it's better to pay for a knowledgeable appraisal than to learn that you have sold a $1,000 item for $100.

## DISPLAYING YOUR COLLECTION

Every collector wants other people to enjoy his or her acquisitions. You may not know how to display your treasures in the most attractive, safe way.

The basis of any display is the relationship of the objects to the space available. If you can afford it and your collection justifies it, you might devote an entire room to your mementos. You would decorate the room in colors compatible with those in your collection. You also would buy such things as back-lighted, recessed cabinets. These would ensure that each item would get maximum exposure.

Most collectors do not have a spare room for their mementos. If you are one of these, you will have to integrate your collection into a room not designed for its display. You will want to place choice items on shelves or in cabinets that do not clash with the room's furniture or colors.

Designing your display should be fun. You can create a beautiful display by following a few simple rules:

**Displaying Small Items**—Small mementos such as prize-fight tickets or buttons are best displayed in groups. Putting them under glass makes such items especially attractive. Try placing your collection in a shadow box on the wall or a similar box mounted under a çoffee table. Be sure to use boxes and cabinets with movable shelves. These will enable you to change the positions of your mementos. Use tiny spotlights and picture lights to emphasize choice examples.

**Displaying Large Items**—Mementos such as duck decoys can be mounted on small individual platforms affixed to a wall.

**Keeping Your Mementos Safe**—This should be a prime consideration. Pieces that could be knocked over or easily removed should be fixed to a base. Pieces that could be damaged by direct exposure to sunlight should be kept in shaded areas.

The more valuable your collection, the more careful you must be when designing your display. If you have questions, consult an experienced decorator.

## STORING SPORTS COLLECTIBLES

You may not be able to display your entire collection at one time. You may have too many pieces or you may not have enough room. In either case, you will have to store part of your collection.

Proper storage is as important as proper display. Unfortunately, only general rules can be provided. The reason is that sports collectibles are made from an enormous variety of materials. Some items are paper, others are wood, ceramic or silver. Use the following rules as guidelines.

**Choose Storage Areas Carefully**—Don't store mementos in damp areas. Avoid putting memorabilia in areas exposed to direct sunlight or sudden temperature changes.

**Prevent Insect Damage**—Insects can damage cloth or paper items. Store these mementos in mothballs or with other anti-insect agents.

**Use Packing Materials**—Wrap fragile pieces in padded packing materials to cushion them from shocks.

Never store metal objects in containers or wrappings that can produce corrosion.

## CLEANING AND REPAIRING COLLECTIBLES

If you have to clean an acquisition, remember that *least is best*. In most cases, use only a mild detergent and warm water. However, don't use water on objects made of paper, cardboard or some types of leather.

Metal cleaners can be used on tarnished brass and copper, and rust remover can be used on iron. However, apply these with care. Always test the surface first to see how the cleaner affects it. Clean only one small area at a time.

After metals, woods and leathers have been cleaned, they can be restored or protected against further deterioration. You can do this by applying a commercial oil or finishing agent. However, don't

experiment! Find out how the product will affect your memento before you apply it. Books on cleaning and restoring antiques can be helpful.

Restoration is controversial. Some collectors don't believe in it. They leave their mementos as they found them. They believe damage and missing pieces are part of the "history" of the object.

Most collectors prefer to restore their acquisitions. However, poorly done restoration work is worse than none at all. If an item is valuable, take it to a professional restorer. Get an estimate first. You may find the cost is too high.

If you think you can do the restoration work yourself, be sure to read about the process first. Work slowly and follow directions carefully. If parts are missing, don't try to guess what they looked like. Find a picture of a complete example.

Restoration work can be fun and can increase the value of a damaged piece. However, it requires skill, patience and time.

## DOING RESEARCH

Some categories of sports memorabilia have been carefully researched. These include duck decoys, sporting firearms and yachting mementos. Many other categories have not been examined in detail.

Most collectors want to know the history of the items they buy. When and where were these mementos made? By whom? If specialized books aren't available for your field, you can uncover much of this information yourself.

Researching sports memorabilia can be as much fun as collecting. Think of it as a treasure hunt. The information you seek is out there somewhere, you just have to find it. When you do, you will experience a special kind of satisfaction. You will probably be the only person in the world to have compiled all this information. This is something you can share with family, friends and other collectors.

Research is a step-by-step process. The first step is to select the piece you want to learn about. Let's assume it is a 20th-century fishing reel. Examine the reel closely. It should have the name and address of a manufacturer stamped somewhere on it. Write to the chamber of commerce or historical society in the town or city where the reel was made. Such organizations often have catalogs and old advertising materials. At the very least, they can tell you whether the firm is in business.

If you live near a large library, look through newspaper files for information on the company. Don't forget to look at the advertisements. They are excellent sources of information.

Libraries can provide other sources, too. Most large cities and towns issued business directories from 1800 until the 1930s or 1940s. These listed active companies. Census records and family histories might also be helpful.

Decoys shaped like frogs are rare. This decoy is especially valuable because it includes the original jigging stick that fishermen used to manipulate the decoy. Made between 1930 and 1940, this example is worth $75 to $135.

Well-carved, painted fish decoys can bring high prices. Top to bottom: The sunfish decoy costs $450 to $550. The largemouth bass decoy is worth $300 to $400. The perchlike decoy was carved by Oscar Petersen of Michigan and is valued at $200 to $300. These decoys were made between 1910 from 1940.

Researching collectibles can be slow and sometimes unrewarding. You may spend hours or days and write a dozen letters to obtain one small bit of information. However, for those who like it, research often becomes one of the most satisfying parts of collecting.

## CATALOGING YOUR COLLECTION

As your collection grows, you should make a catalog or list of what you own. This will enable you to find information quickly. It will make it easy for you to check where and when you bought each item and what you paid for it.

The best way to catalog a collection is to use a system of numbers or letters or both. The only thing you will need is a blank record book.

Place a number or a code that combines letters and numbers on each acquisition. You can write the number on a small sticker and put it on the bottom of the item. Enter the same number or code in your record book. Next to the number or code in the book, list all the information you have about the object. This should include where, when and from whom you bought it. Be sure to record how much you paid for it. Also include anything the person you bought it from told you about the item.

Make a note about the condition of the piece when you bought it. Then record any restoration work you did.

Write down any other relevant information, including the results of your research. Include a photograph of the item if you have one.

If you sell a memento, record the buyer's name, the date and the price. This will give you a permanent record of every item that enters your collection.

It is impossible to remember all this information indefinitely. With your record book, you can quickly find any data you need about any piece. Just look at the number or code on the item, then refer to your record book. Many collectors put this information on home computers!

## PHOTOGRAPHING YOUR COLLECTION

Photographs are an important part of your record book. If you take your book with you on buying trips, photographs can ensure that you don't purchase duplicates of items you already have. This can be a serious problem for people whose collections include hundreds of pieces.

Photographs also provide security. If your collection is valuable, you will want to insure it. Most insurance companies request a photograph of each object to be insured. Even if the company doesn't want photographs of your mementos, such pictures can be useful. They can help support a claim for loss or damage.

You can hire a professional photographer to take pictures of your collection, but they often charge high fees. It might cost several thousand dollars to photograph 200 or 300 pieces. Fortunately, you can do the photography yourself.

You will need a good 35mm camera. Polaroid cameras are not recommended, because the pictures they produce are not sharp enough. You will also need a piece of white cloth or paper to use as a backdrop.

Photograph one item at a time. Place the item against the backdrop and make an exposure. Your pictures may not be artistic, but they will do the job.

## INSURANCE AND SECURITY

As the value of your collection increases, you should insure it.

**Appraisals**—Insurance companies usually want an *appraisal,* or estimate, of the value of each item in your collection. You can obtain an appraisal from a professional antique dealer or auctioneer for a fee. Try to hire someone who handles objects similar to those in your collection. Such a person probably knows current market values.

Send one copy of the appraisal to the insurance company. Keep another copy at home. You may want to put it in your record book.

Security is becoming a problem for collectors. Enthusiasts have always had to worry about fires, earthquakes, falling trees and hurricanes. Now they must also be concerned with theft.

**Home Security Systems**—These systems are expensive but are sometimes advisable. If your collection is very valuable, you should consider installing one.

Make sure your doors and windows are always securely fastened. Alert trustworthy neighbors when you leave home for an extended period. Dogs are helpful, but the best watchdog is a concerned neighbor.

Be discreet about telling people about your fabulous collection. An appearance on a local television program or an article in a hometown newspaper can lead to tragedy. More than once, such an appearance or article has been followed by a burglary.

## LEARNING TO BE LUCKY

Acquiring and maintaining a collection may seem like a great deal of work. However, your efforts are part of a fascinating process.

Collecting will help you learn more about the world. As you research the objects you buy, you will also acquire information about how the United States developed. Each collectible has its own story, which involves how people lived and what they did with their leisure time. The more you learn, the more knowledgeable you will become. Successful collecting results partly from luck, but in the long run, the knowledgeable collector is the luckiest.

# SPORTS MEMORABILIA COLLECTOR'S RECORD BOOK

CODE # _____

SPORT _____

DATE OF PURCHASE _____

CONDITION _____

PURCHASE PRICE _____


ASSESSED VALUE _____

SOURCE OF ACQUISITION _____

_____


MANUFACTURER (IF KNOWN) _____


DESCRIPTION

    SIZE _____

    COLOR _____

    SHAPE _____

    LABEL _____

    MATERIALS USED _____

    DISTINGUISHING MARKS _____

    _____


RESEARCH

    PUBLICATIONS OR EXPERTS CONSULTED _____

    _____

    _____

    RESULTS OF RESEARCH _____

    _____

    _____


NOTES _____

_____

_____


Make copies of this page to create your own record book.

# Price Guide

No matter which category of sports memorabilia you choose, you will need to know prevailing prices for the items you want. This will ensure that you never pay too much for a memento, or sell it for too little. Part of the fun of collecting is learning how to determine price.

It is very difficult to establish values for sports mementos. Hundreds of items can be classified as sports memorabilia. Furthermore, some categories do not interest many collectors. These factors make it difficult to set firm prices.

Remember that this price guide is just that—a guide. To use it wisely, you must understand how prices for sports memorabilia are established.

## SUPPLY AND DEMAND

The laws of supply and demand determine prices. There are two basic laws. First, a rare item is usually worth more than a plentiful one. Second, an item many people are interested in is more valuable than one few people care about.

Prices change continually. Sports memorabilia are not like shoes or watches. When a dealer sells a choice piece, he can't simply order a new one. It may be years before he finds a piece similar to the one he sold. And when he does, the price will no longer be the same.

Cost—This is just one factor that affects how much a dealer charges for an item. He must also add something for overhead, restoration and profit. The profit margin is usually 15% to 25%.

If you consider all these factors, you can see why prices vary. The price you pay for an item will depend on when, where and from whom you buy it.

Because of this situation, the guide in this book gives you a range of prices, such as $25 to $40. This range reflects the highest and lowest prevailing prices.

Any guide can cover only some of the sports mementos available. The price guide in this book lists key examples in each category. Use these prices to get an idea of the value of comparable pieces.

## OTHER FACTORS

The prices given here are for examples in good condition. Such pieces show normal wear, are undamaged, have not been restored and have no missing parts. Damage, missing parts, significant loss of paint or finish, or extensive restoration will lower the price of any collectible. Never pay more than 25% to 75% of the average retail price for a damaged piece. You should never purchase a seriously damaged piece unless it is so rare that you are unlikely to find another.

Restoration—Restored or repainted collectibles are worth less than pieces that have not needed repairs—unless the buyer doesn't know the work has been done. Fortunately, few collectors do restoration work.

Numerous examples of sports memorabilia are available, and prices for many items are still low. You should not have to buy repaired examples.

Reproductions—Few copies of sports items are being made. Therefore, you will not have the problems confronting collectors of other antiques. Bottle and toy collectors must carefully appraise potential acquisitions to make sure such items are not inexpensive reproductions.

Very few sports collectibles are handled by dealers or sold at auction. Items associated with less-popular sports such as bullfighting and croquet are seldom found through these sources. This is unfortunate, because auction prices are usually a reliable gauge of current market prices.

Setting a Limit—Sometimes a dealer doesn't know how much to ask for a sports memento. He may ask the highest price he can think of. Don't go along with this practice. Use the price guidelines in this book and your own good judgment. If the dealer wants too much, walk away. You will probably find a similar example before long.

Remember that the field of sports memorabilia is new. As a collector, you are helping establish prices. The amount you pay today will help determine the amount you pay tomorrow. Let's say a dealer wants $150 for an ordinary baseball bat made in the 1920s. This price is very high. If you agree to pay it, the dealer will charge at least that much the next time he gets a similar bat. Don't pay too much. High prices make it hard for you and other collectors to get what you want.

These handmade casting reels were produced from 1880 to 1900. Left to right: J. F. and B. F. Meek, Frankfort, Ky., $600 to $700; Horton Manufacturing Co., Bristol, Conn., $100 to $135; B.C. Milam, Frankfort, Ky., $450 to $600; George W. Gayles & Son, Frankfort, Ky., $700 to $800. Because so many casting reels were made in Kentucky, they are often called *Kentucky reels.*

Casting reels made between 1940 and 1950 are inexpensive and offer opportunities for new collectors. Left: Anodized aluminum Jorgensen 115, $5 to $10. Right: Hendryx reel, made between 1920 and 1940, is worth $25 to $35.

Wood lures made from the 1920s to the 1940s are popular with collectors of bait-casting lures. Clockwise from top: Surfster with original box, Creek Chub Bait Co., Garrett, Ind., $45 to $55; Rush Tango, $20 to $35; Minnow with fore and aft spinners, James Heddon & Sons, Dowagiac, Mich., $35 to $60; multiwobbler in red, $40 to $65; Pflueger Surprise Minnow, $20 to $35.

Most plastic lures from the 1950s are inexpensive. Clockwise from upper left: Glo-Lite Mouse, William Shakespeare Jr. Co., Kalamazoo, Mich., $3 to $6; Little Lure Frog, Heddon, $40 to $60; Miracle Lure, Wright & McGill, $5 to $10; Kick-N-Kackle, Orchard Industries, $6 to $12; frog-form kicker, Jenson, $10 to $15. The Heddon Little Lure Frog was one of the first plastic baits.

This 1887 issue of *The American Angler* magazine costs $10 to $15. The low price reflects the magazine's lack of color illustrations. Most collectible magazines date from 1920 to 1950. Copies of *Sports Afield, Field & Stream* and similar publications sell for $2 to $20, depending on rarity, reputation of the cover artist and condition.

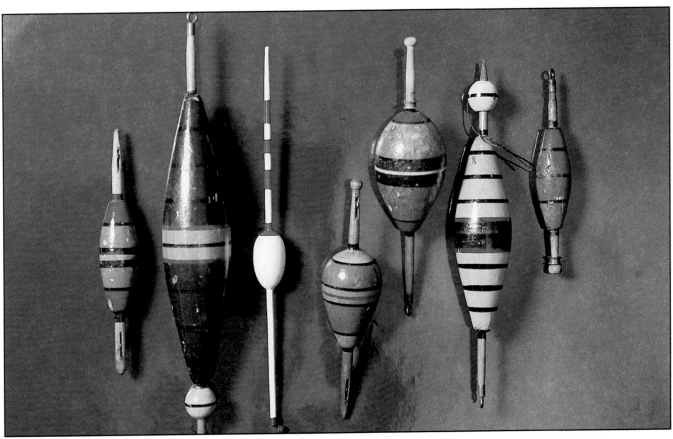

These cork-and-wood bobbers used in bait fishing were made between 1900 and 1940. They cost $3 to $20, depending on size and color. These items are popular with decorators and folk art enthusiasts.

These mementos include a kidney-shaped bait box, $10 to $25; rare copper minnow bucket, $25 to $75; gaff, $30 to $45; minnow box, $20 to $30; fish net, $15 to $30; early tackle box, $30 to $45; and a rare glass minnow trap, Orvis, $65 to $85. Handmade equipment usually brings the highest prices.

Advertising materials, such as this three-dimensional Pflueger sign from the 1950s, are popular with collectors. This piece is worth $35 to $50.

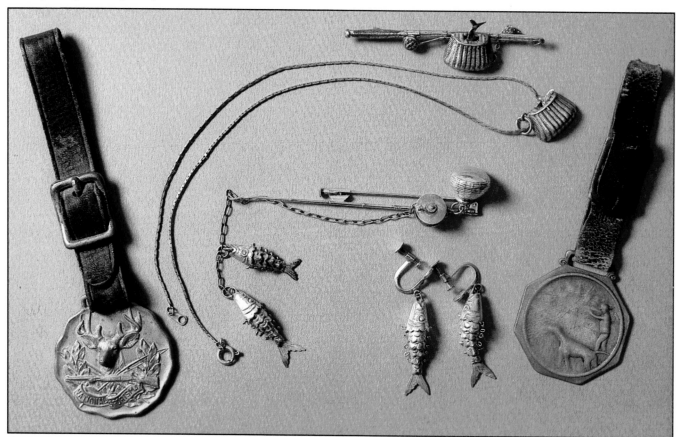

You can assemble an interesting collection of jewelry with fishing themes. Clockwise from top: Pin shaped like a rod and creel, $75 to $95; silver pendant shaped like a creel, $60 to $75; brass watch fob advertising *Sportsman's Digest,* $20 to $25; sterling-silver earrings and brooch, $125 to $150; National Sportsman brass watch fob, $35 to $45.

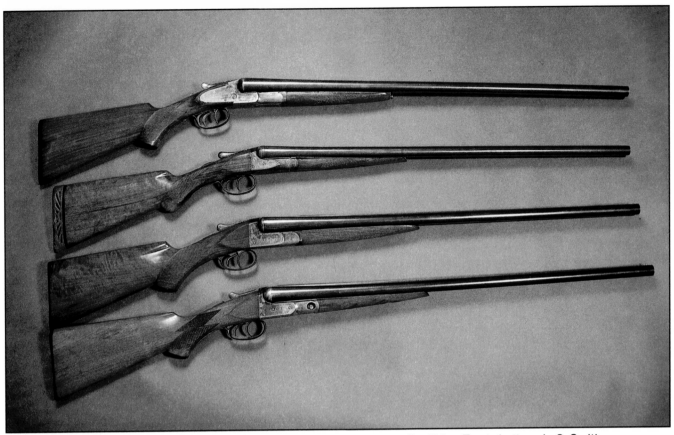

These 20th-century shotguns by well-known manufacturers are prime collectibles. Top to bottom: L. C. Smith Field Grade 12-gauge shotgun, $500 to $600; A. H. Fox A Grade 16-gauge shotgun, $600 to $700; Ithaca Field Grade 12-gauge shotgun, $500 to $600; Parker VH Grade 12-gauge shotgun, $650 to $750.

Hunting knives are very interesting collectibles. Top to bottom: Small bowie knife, $70 to $95; sheath knife, Marble, $30 to $35; wide-blade canoe knife, Remington, $40 to $55; German knife with screwdriver, saw and other utensils, Solingen, $85 to $110; small woods knife, Cattaragus Cutlery, $20 to $30.

Individual shotgun shells are collectible, especially early brass-cased examples. Unusually large or small shells are also valuable. These shells, by Remington and Winchester, were made from 1880 to 1920. They cost $3 to $15 each. Shells that have been fired are much less valuable than unfired examples.

Magazines devoted to hunting are usually inexpensive. Clockwise, from upper left: Stoeger's *The Shooter's Bible,* 1942, $17 to $22; hunting edition of *Field and Stream,* 1902, $20 to $30; *Gun Digest,* 1954, $5 to $8; *American Rifleman,* May 1981, $1 to $2.

Cattle horns are excellent bargains. These cost $5 to $8 each. The African antelope skull is worth $200 to $250.

Numerous types of hunting and fishing license buttons are available. The 1917 New York State button shown here is a bargain at $70 to $85. It was the state's first license button. Most pre-1930 buttons are worth about $20. Examples made after 1930 cost $10 to $20.

Contemporary miniature decoys are made to please collectors, not to fool ducks. These examples are four inches to six inches long. They include a pheasant, mallard and sea gull. Such decoys are a good investment at $30 to $45 each. Examples by well-known carvers are more expensive.

This baseball glove made by H. J. Wilson Co., Baton Rouge, La., was made from 1950 to 1960 and costs $30 to $40. The baseball with the facsimile signature of Ford Frick was made by Spalding, Chicopee, Mass., and is worth $10 to $15. The baseball with the genuine autograph of Marty Marion costs $35 to $50.

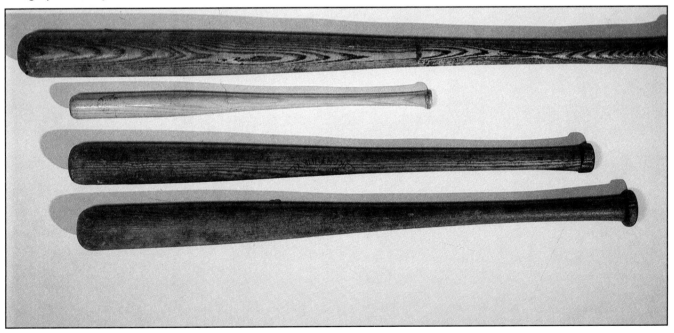

Old baseball bats have little value unless they were used by an important player. The small example, second from the top is an early Little League Louisville Slugger. It was manufactured from 1945 to 1955 and costs $15 to $20. Below it is a New York Yankees souvenir miniature made between 1960 and 1970. It is worth $3 to $5. The other bats, made between 1930 and 1945, are $5 to $10 each.

Press passes are popular and hard-to-find baseball ephemera. Season passes are worth $15 to $45, depending on age. World Series passes, which are rare, bring $35 to $75 each.

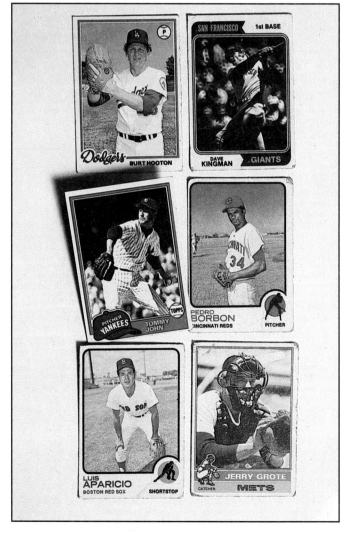

These baseball cards by the Topps Chewing Gum Co., Brooklyn, New York, were made between 1972 and 1980. They cost 25 cents to 50 cents each. Topps has long been the most prolific baseball-card manufacturer. These examples include player cards of stars such as Tommy John and Dave Kingman.

The large plastic football helmet was an ice-cream container and is worth $1 to $2. The smaller examples were sold in vending machines and cost 35 cents to 55 cents each.

Felt football pennants are appealing and easy to find. Most college pennants don't interest collectors, but professional examples such as these are worth $3 to $15.

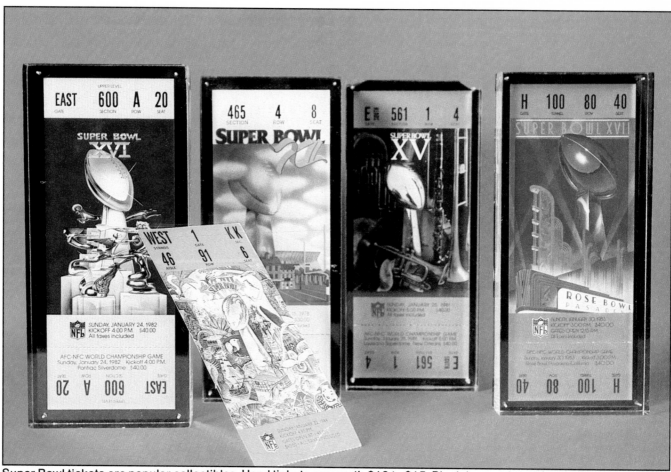

Super Bowl tickets are popular collectibles. Used tickets are worth $10 to $15. Plexiglas-enclosed facsimiles are worth $20 to $25.

Various types of professional football collectibles are available. Clockwise, from upper left: a Super Bowl XV belt buckle, $20 to $30; Super Bowl XV shoulder patch, $12 to $18; book of matches shaped like a helmet with the logo of the New York Jets, $3 to $5; Super Bowl XV ballpoint pen, $10 to $13; Super Bowl XVII key chain, $10 to $15.

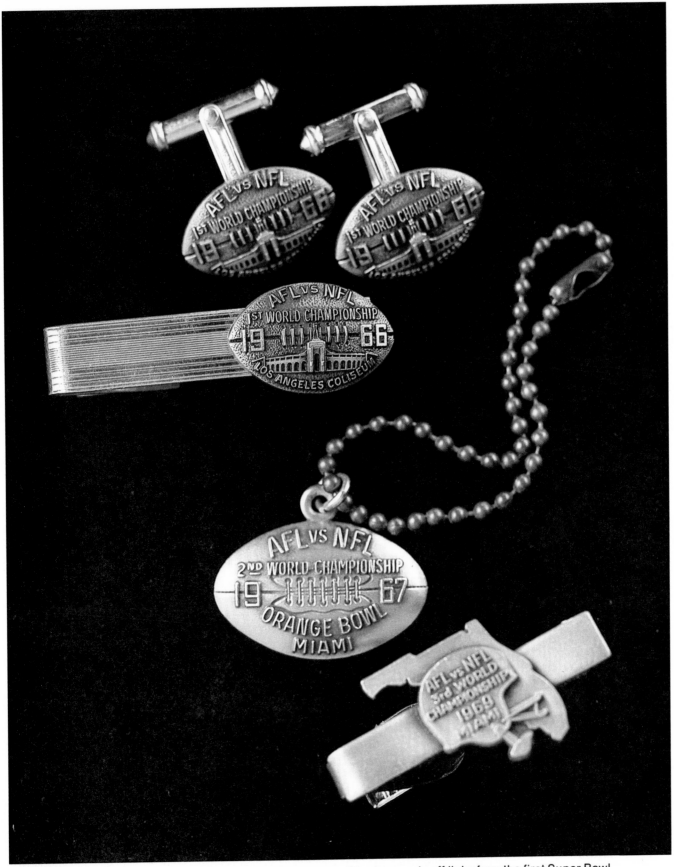

Super Bowl jewelry is popular and hard to find. Top to bottom: Tie clasp and cuff links from the first Super Bowl, in 1966, $150 to $235 a set; key chain from the 1967 game, $50 to $65; tie clasp from the 1969 game, $65 to $85. All are gold-filled.

Novelty football cards such as these cost 25 cents to 75 cents each, depending on condition, popularity and rarity.

These basketball cards, featuring such popular National Basketball Association stars as Dave Cowens and Nate Archibald, were made between 1976 and 1977. They cost 20 cents to 25 cents each. Basketball cards, less popular than baseball and football cards, are a good investment.

These early tennis rackets, made from 1920 to 1930, are worth $25 to $45 each. Clockwise from left: A Pennant, an early Spalding, a Champion and a Star. Such rackets are easy to find and inexpensive.

Early tennis balls are smaller than those used today. These examples are especially valuable because they were found in their original packing box. They were manufactured between 1910 and 1925. The balls cost $3 to $5 apiece, or $65 to $80 a set.

This oil painting of *racquets,* a forerunner of modern squash and tennis, is worth more than $1,000. It was produced between 1850 and 1860. Always have an expert evaluate a 19th-century oil painting of a tennis match. Such paintings are rare.

Watch fobs, medallions and badges awarded to golfers or used to indicate golf-club membership are collectible. These brass, bronze and white-metal examples, made between 1920 and 1940, cost $5 to $15 each. Silver examples are more expensive.

Numerous smoking and drinking articles associated with golf are available. Clockwise, from top: Wood cigarette box with golfing print, 1930 to 1940, $25 to $35; chrome cocktail mixers, stirrer and double jigger, 1930 to 1940, $35 to $50 a set; celluloid swizzle sticks shaped like golf clubs, 1925 to 1935, $20 to $30 a set; glass ashtray with golf-course layout, 1973, $5 to $10.

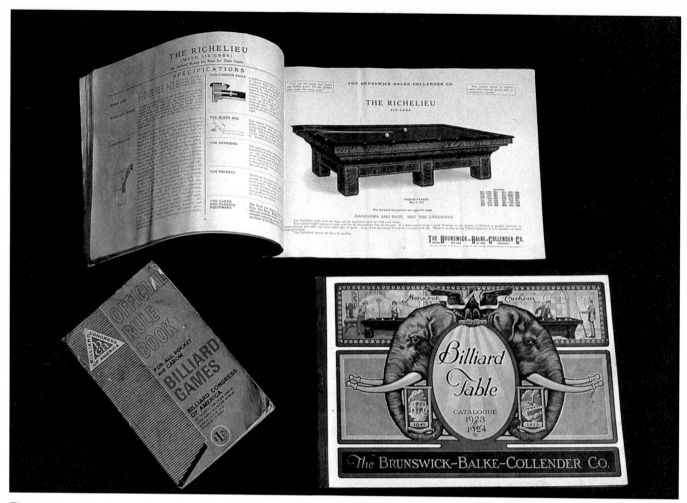

These types of billiards ephemera interest collectors. Clockwise, from top: Brunswick-Balke-Collander catalog, 1912, $125 to $175; Brunswick-Balke-Collander catalog, 1923, $125 to $175; Billiard Congress of America rule book, 1965, $10 to $15.

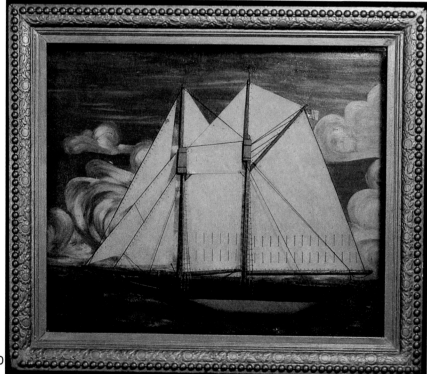

Among the most interesting sailing memorabilia are half-models of racing boats mounted under glass. This schooner model, made between 1880 and 1900, is worth $350 to $500.

Advertising posters featuring important sailing events, such as the America's Cup, are popular with young collectors. This well-mounted example costs $65 to $85. An unmounted example is worth $30 to $40.

These skiing shoulder patches cost $2 to $4 each. Such patches first appeared in the 1950s, but most collectible examples were made between 1970 and 1980.

Children's tricycles from the 1880s cost $300 to $600 each. You can buy tricycles made between 1920 and 1930 for $35 to $100.

# Bibliography

This recommended list of books can help when you research sports collectibles. Books marked with * are out of print and probably won't be readily available at bookstores. Books marked with † are privately printed or published by small, regional publishers. These too may be difficult to find. Therefore, you should supplement this list with books available from local libraries or used bookstores.

* Blackmore, Howard L. *Hunting Weapons.* New York: Walker, 1971.

† Chamberlain, R.H. *Early Loading Tools and Bullet Molds.* Porterville, CA: privately published, 1970.

* Colio, Quintana. *American Decoys.* Ephrata, PA: Science Press, 1972.

* Curtis, Capt. P.A. *Guns and Gunning.* New York, NY: Alfred Knopf, 1946.

* Datig, F.A. *Cartridges for Collectors,* vols. I-III. Los Angeles, CA: Borden, 1965-67.

* Elman, Robert. *The Great American Shooting Prints.* New York, NY: Alfred Knopf, 1972.

Erbe, Ron. *The American Premium Guide to Baseball Cards, 1880-1981.* Florence, AL: Books Americana, 1982.

* Ernest, Adele. *The Art of the Decoy.* New York, NY: Bramhill House, 1965.

Fleckenstein, Henry A. *Decoys of the Mid-Atlantic Region.* Exton, PA: Schiffer Publishing, 1979.

Fleyderman, Norman. *Guide to Antique American Firearms.* Northfield, IL: Digest Books, 1980.

* Fox, Charles K. *The Book of Lures.* Rockville Centre, NY: Fresler Press, 1975.

Hudgeons, Thomas E., III. *Official Price Guide to Baseball Cards.* Orlando, FL: House of Collectibles, 1984.

Hudgeons, Thomas E., III. *Official Price Guide to Football Cards.* Orlando, FL: House of Collectibles, 1984.

Hudgeons, Thomas E., III, ed. *Official Price Guide to Sports Collectibles.* Orlando, FL: House of Collectibles, 1984.

* Hughes, B. R. *The Gun Digest Book of Knives.* Northfield, IL: Digest Books, 1973.

Ketchum, William C., Jr. *Western Memorabilia: Collectibles of the Old West.* Maplewood, NJ: Hammond, Inc., 1980.

Kimball, Art, and Kimball, Scott. *Collecting Old Fishing Tackle.* New York: Aardvark Publications, 1980.

* Latham, Sid. *Great Sporting Posters of the Golden Age.* Harrisburg, PA: Stackpole Books, 1978.

Liu, Allan J. *The American Sporting Collector's Handbook.* Tulsa, OK: Winchester Press, 1982.

Luckey, Carl F. *Old Fishing Lures and Tackle.* Decatur, IN: American Books, 1980.

* Mackey, William J., Jr. *American Bird Decoys.* New York, NY: E.P. Dutton, 1965.

McClane, A. J. *McClane's New Standard Fishing Encyclopedia.* New York: Holt, Rinehart & Winston, 1974.

Melner, Samuel, and Kessler, Herman, eds. *Great Fishing Tackle Catalogs of the Golden Age.* New York, NY: Crown, 1972.

O'Connor, Jack. *The Shotgun Book.* New York, NY: Alfred Knopf, 1978.

* Patterson, Jerry S. *Antiques of Sport.* New York, NY: Crown, 1975.

* Riling, R. *The Powder Flask Book.* New York, NY: Bonanza Books, 1953.

* Starr, George Ross. *Decoys of the Atlantic Flyway.* New York, NY: Winchester Press, 1974.

* Suehsdorf, A. D. *The Great American Baseball Scrapbook.* New York, NY: Random House, 1978.

* Sugar, Bert R. *The Nostalgia Collectors Bible.* New York: Quick Fox, 1981.

Taylor, John. *Golf Collector's Price Guide.* Bucks, England: St. Giles, 1984.

# Index

**A**

Aaron, Hank, 16
Abbey & Imbrie, 33
Abdul-Jabbar, Kareem, 23
advertising, 68
*American Angler, 77*
American Basketball Association (ABA), 22
*American Football, 17*
American Football League (AFL), 18
*American Rifleman, 80*
America's Cup, 6, 56, *93*
ammunition, *39,* 40, 42
  boxes, 40
appraisals, 6, 72
Arbogast casting lures, 35
archery collectibles, 55
Archibald, Nate, 88
Arkansas toothpicks, 6, 40
arrow bolts, 6
arrows, 55
auctions, 69
Austin, Tracy, 30

**B**

Babe Ruth, 12, 16
badminton collectibles, 55
bag, 6
bobbers, 6, *77*
*Baseball Blue Book,* 12
baseball collectibles, 11-17, *11-16, 83,* 8 4, 85
  cards, 12-16, *13, 14, 15, 84*
*Baseball Digest,* 12
*Baseball Magazine,* 12
*Baseball Yearbook,* 12
basketball collectibles, 22-23, *22, 23, 88*
batteries, 6, 48
battery decoys, 6, 48
*Beadle Baseball Guide,* 12
beaters, 6, 37
Bergman, Ray, 36
bicycling collectibles, 51-54
  ordinary, 8, *8*
  tricycles, *93*
  velocipedes, 9
billiards collectibles, 55-56, *55, 92*
bird (See *shuttlecocks*)
boating collectibles, 56, *92*
bobbers, 6, *77*
bolts, 6
bone crusher, 6, 51
*Book of the Black Bass, The,* 36
bore, 6
Borg, Bjorn, *63*
Bowie knife, 6, 40, *79*
bowling collectibles, 56-57
Bowman Co., 16, 18, 23
bows, 55
  crossbows, 6, 55
boxing collectibles, 57
Bradley, Bill, 22
brassies, 6, 25
breech-loading firearms, 6, 38
brick, 6
Bristol Steel Fishing Rods, *36*
Brown, Jim, 17
Browning (firearms manufacturer), 38
Brunswick-Balke-Collander, 92
Budge, Don, 28
Buel, J. T., 35
Buffalo guns, 6, 37
bullfighting collectibles, 57, *59*
bull's-eye, 6

**C**

Camillus Cutlery, 40
Camp, Walter, 17
Canadian Football League, 18
cane (Asian bamboo), 6, 32
cape, matador's (See *capote, muleta*)
**capote,** 6
cards, collector's (See specific sport)
Carson, Kit, 38

cartridges, 6, 40
Carvel ice-cream container tops, 23
casting lures, 6, 34-35, *35, 76*
  plugs, 8, 35
  spinner, 9, 35
  spoon, 9, 35
casting reels, 6, *75*
  multiplying reel, 8
casting rods, 6, 33
cataloging a collection, 72, 73
catgut, 28
Cattaragus Cutlery, *79*
Chamberlain, Wilt, 23
Chicago Cubs, 16
Clark, Robert, 25
cleaning collectibles, *64,* 70
closed-face reels, 6
clubs, golf (See *golf collectibles*)
Cobb, Ty, 11
*Colt on the Trail, 39*
*Compleat Angler, The,* 36
composition, 6
confidence decoys, 6, 46
Cooper, James Fenimore, 37
courting game, the, 9, 57
Cowens, Dave, 23, *88*
Creek Club Bait Co., 35, *76*
creels, 6, *34,* 36
crop, riding, 9
croquet collectibles, 57, *57*
crossbows, 6, 55
Crowell, A. Elmer, *10,* 48
cues, billiards, 6, *55,* 56
Currier & Ives prints, *4,* 36, 56, *56*

**D**

Dallas Cowboys cheerleaders, 18
Davis Cup Contest (1923), *31*
dealers, 68, 69
decoys
  battery, 6, 48
  carved, 48
  confidence, 6, 46
  duck, 6, 44, 46, *46, 47*
  factory-made, 48
  fish, 49-50, *71*
  floating, 7
  frog, *71*
  goose, 47
  how made, 46-48
  miniature, *82*
  owl, 48
  sea-duck, 44, *44*
  shore-bird, 9, 10, *45,* 46-48
  silhouette, 9, 47
  working, 9
Diamond Match Co., 16
displaying, 60, 62, 69-70
Dodge Trophy Co., 26
Donruss Co., The, 16
Dorsett, Tony, 17
Doubleday, Abner, 11
drivers, 6, 25
dry flies, *34,* 35
duck decoys (See *decoys*)
duck stamps, 7, *40,* 42

**E**

ebonized, 7
Edwards Rod Co., *32*
epee, 7, 57
ephemera, 7, 12
error cards, 7, 16
Erving, Julius ("Dr. J"), 22

**F**

facsimile signatures, 7, 12, *14*
fair, 7
fanzine, 7
Federal Endangered Species Act, 42
Federal Migratory Bird Hunting Stamps, *40,* 42
fencing collectibles, 57

*Field and Stream,* 36, *77, 80*
finding collectibles, 66-69
fine, 7
firearms, sporting, 37-38, *79*
  famous manufacturers of, 38
  handguns, 7, 37-38
  long guns, 37-38
  Kentucky rifles, 7, *37,* 38
fish decoys, 49-50, *71*
fishing collectibles, 32-36, *32-36, 62, 78, 82*
Fleer Corp., 16, 18, 23
flies, 7, *34,* 35
flintlocks, 7, 38
fly reels, 7, *33,* 34
fly rods, 7, 32-33, *32*
floating decoy, 7
foil, 7, 57
football collectibles, 17-21, *18-21, 86, 88*
Fox, A. H., *79*
fox-hunting collectibles, 58
Frick, Ford, *83*
frog decoys, *71*

**G**

game, 7
gauge, green's-level, 9, 25
gauge, shot-gun, 7
Gayles, George W., & Son, *75*
Gehrig, Lou, 12
giveaway, 7
Golcher, Joseph, *37*
Gold Coin Chewing Tobacco Co., 14
golf collectibles, 25-27, *25-27, 91*
*Golf Digest,* 27
Gonzalez, Pancho, 28
good, 7
Goodwin, Phillip R., 42
Goodwin & Co., 14
goose decoys, 47
Goudey Gum Co., 14, 18
go-withs, 7
green's-level gauges, 7, 25
*Gun Digest,* 80
gunning equipment, 7, 38-40
guns (See *firearms, sporting*)

**H**

hallmark, 7
Hambletonian, 4
handguns, 7, 37-38
Hardy Bros., *33*
hatchlock, 7
Heddon, James, & Sons, 33, 35, *76*
Hemingway, Ernest, 57
Hendryx casting reel, *75*
Henshall, James A., 36
high-ticket items, 7, 60
Hillerich & Bradsby, 11
Horrocks-Ibbotson Co., *33*
horse racing and riding collectibles, 58
Horton Manufacturing Co., *36, 75*
how-to book, 7
Huddle football game, *18*
Hudson, Ira, 64
Hunt, Lynn Bogue, 42
*Hunting and Fishing,* 36
hunting collectibles, 37-43, *39, 41, 62*
hunting knives, 6, 40, *79*

**I**

ice-skating collectibles, 51-52, 54
ice-hockey collectibles, 24-25, *24*
*Illustrated Football Annual,* 17
insurance and security, 72
Ithaca (firearms manufacturer), 38
Iver Johnson, 38
Ivory, 7

**J**

Jack Gordon Special Putter, *25*
jigs, 7, 49-50, *49*
John, Tommy, *84*
Jorgensen casting reel, *75*

*Judge,* 55
*Just Fishing,* 36

**K**
Kentucky reels, 7, 34, *75*
Kentucky rifles, 7, *37,* 38
Kingman, Dave, *84*
knives, hunting, 6, 40, *79*

**L**
leg, 7
Leonard, Hiram, 60
Leonard, H. L., Co., 32, *32, 33*
license buttons, *82*
licenses, hunting, 42
Lincoln, Joseph (Joe), 48
*Little Red Book of Baseball,* 12
long guns, 7, 37-38
Louis, Joe, 57
Louisville Slugger bats, 11, *83*
lure, 8 (See also *casting lures*)
Lyman gun sights catalog, *39*

**M**
MacGregor putter, *25*
man traps, 8, 37
Mantle, Mickey, 16
Marble (manufacturer), *79*
Marion, Marty, *83*
Maris, Roger, 12
Marlin Fire Arms, 38, *39*
Mason Decoy Factory, 48
matchlock, 38
Mays, Willie, 12
medals, 8
Meek, J. F. & B. F., 34, *75*
Meisselbach, A. F., Manufacturing Co., *33,* 34
Milam, B. C., *75*
mint, 8
Mitchell, William, 32
models, boat, 56, *92*
Montague City Rod and Reel Co., 33
Mossberg (firearms manufacturer), 38
*muleta,* 8
multiplying reels, 8, 34
muzzle-loading firearms, 8, 38

**N**
Naismith, James, 22
National Basketball Association (NBA), 22
National Chicle Co., 18
National Collegiate Athletic Association (NCAA), 22
*National Collegiate Athletic Association Official Football Guide,* 17
National Football League (NFL), 61, *67*
National Horse Show, 58
National Invitational Tournament (NIT), 22
New York Yankees, *14, 83*
nine pins, 8, 56

**O**
O PEE CHEE Co., 18
Orchard Industries, 76
ordinary, 8, *8* (See *penny farthing*)
Osthaus, Edmund, 42
Orvis Co., Inc., The, *32, 33,* 34, 64, *78*
Outerbridge, Mary Ewing, 28
owl decoys, 48

**P**
Parker Guns, *39, 79*
Parkhurst, 24
Paw Paw casting lures, 35
Payne, Edward, 60
peeps, 8, 46
pennants, 8, *12, 85*
penny farthing, 8, 52
percussion cap firearms, 8, 38
Peters (firearms manufacturer), *39*
Petersen, Oscar, *71*
Pflueger Enterprises Manufacturing Co., 34, *76, 78*
photographing a collection, 72
plains rifles, 8, 38
plinkers, 8, 40
plugs, 8, 35, *35*

poaching, 8, 37
pocket cap, 8, 33
polo collectibles, 58
pool (billiards) collectibles, 55-56, *55, 92*
*poona,* 8, 55
poor, 8
powder flasks, *37*
powder horns, 8, 38, *38*
press passes, pins and tags, *22, 61, 84*
*Prolog,* 63
provenance, 8
punch board, 8

**R**
racing silks, 9, 58
rack, 9
rackets
    badminton, 55
    tennis, 28, *28, 29,* 30, *89*
racquets, 9, *90*
rapier, 9, 57
Rawlings Sporting Goods Co., 11, 17
reels, fishing
    casting, 6, 34, *75*
    closed-face, 6
    fly, *33,* 34
    Kentucky, 7
    multiplying, 8, 34
    saltwater, 34
    single-action, 9, 34
    spinning, 9, 34
    spinning, 9, 34
    wood, *33*
Remington Arms Co., 38, *39,* 40, 42, *79, 80*
repairing collectibles, *66,* 70
Resch, Glen ("Chico"), *24*
researching collectibles, 70, 72, 73
riding crop, 9
rifles, 37-38
    buffalo guns, 6, 37
    Kentucky, 7, *37,* 38
    plains, 8, 38
rifling, 9
rodeo collectibles, 58
*Rod and Gun,* 36
rods, fishing
    casting, 6, 33
    fly, 7, 32-33, *32*
    saltwater, 33
    spin-casting, 33
    spinning, 9
roller polo, 9
roller-skating collectibles, 51, 52, *53,* 54, *54*
run, 9, 12
Russel, J., & Co., 40

**S**
saber, 9, 57
sailing collectibles, 56, *56, 92, 93*
saltwater reels, 34
saltwater rods, 33
Savage (firearms manufacturer), 38
Sayers, Gale, *18*
Schoenheider, Charles, 48
sea-duck decoys (See *decoys*)
Shakespeare, William, Jr., Co., 34, *76*
*Shooter's Bible, The,* 80
shore-bird decoys (See *decoys*)
shot shells, 9, *39,* 40, *80*
shotguns, *79* (See *firearms, sporting*)
Shourds, Harry V., 48
show-riding collectibles, 58
shuttlecocks, 9, 55
silhouette decoys, 9, 47-48
single-action reels, 9, 34
skating collectibles
    ice, 51, 52, 54
    roller, 51, 52, *53,* 54, *54*
skiing collectibles, 51, 52, 54, *54, 93*
Smith, L. C., *79*
soccer collectibles, 58
Solingen (cutlery manufacturer), *79*
South Bend Tackle Co., 33, 34, 64

Spalding, 11, 12, 17, *83, 89*
Spalding Golf Museum, 25
*Spalding's Football Guide,* 17
spears, fishing, 49-50, *50*
spin-casting rods, 33
spinners, 9, 35, *35*
spinning lures, 9
spinning reels, 9, 34
spinning rods, 9 33
spoons (bait), 9, 35, *35*
spoons (golf), 9, 25
sporting artist, 9
sporting firearms (See *firearms, sporting*)
*Sporting News,* 12
*Sports Afield,* 77
*Sports Kings* cards, 18
Stanley Cup, 24
stars baseball cards, 16
Stevens, H. A., Factory, 28
stickup decoys, 9, 46
stirrups, 9
storing collectibles, 60, 62, *68,* 70
Strater & Sohier, 45
stymie markers, 9, 25
suit of lights, 9
sulkies, 9, 58
Super Bowl collectibles, *17, 19, 20, 86, 87* (See *football collectibles*)
swap fests, 9

**T**
tack, 9
tackle, fishing, 9, *34,* 36, *78*
taxidermy, 36, 42
team sports, 9
tennis collectibles, 28-31, *28-31, 89, 90*
Theismann, Joe, 17
3-D Super Star cards, *14*
Tilden, Bill, *31*
tin decoys, 47
tip ups, 9, 36
Topps Chewing Gum Co., *15,* 16, 18, *19,* 23, *23,* 24, 57, *84*
*traje de luces* (See *suit of lights*)
traps, man, 8
tricycles, *93*
trophies, 9
    fishing, 36
    game, 38, 42, *43, 81*
trout flies, *34*
*True Football Yearbook,* 17
Twain, Mark, 52

**U**
Union Hardware Co., *53*

**V**
velocipedes, 9, 51
Vom Hofe, Edward and Julius, *33,* 34

**W**
Wagner, Honus, 14
Walton, Izaak, 36
Ward, Lemuel, 4, 48
Ward, Steve, 48
Washington, George, 32
West, Jerry, 22, 23
wheel lock, 9, 38
wheel skating, 9
Wheeler, Charles E. "Shang", *47,* 48
wheelmen, 9, 51
*Who's Who in Baseball,* 12
Wildfowler Decoy Co., 48
Williams, Ted, 12
Wilson, H. J., Co., 11, 17, *83*
Winchester Group, 38, *39,* 42, *80*
Wingfield, Major Walter C., 28
working decoy, 9
*World Series Record Book,* 12
*World Tennis,* 30
Wright & McGill, 33, *76*

**Y**
yachting collectibles, 56, *56*